Quilt &
Embellish
in One Step!

C&T PUBLISHING INC.

LINDA POTTER

Text © 2004 Linda Potter
Artwork © 2004 C&T Publishing, Inc.

Publisher: Amy Marson
Editorial Director: Gailen Runge
Acquisitions Editor: Jan Grigsby
Developmental Editor: Candie Frankel
Technical Editor: Sara Kate MacFarland
Copyeditor/Proofreader: Eva Simoni Erb, Wordfirm
Cover Designer: Kristen Yenche
Design Director: Dave Nash
Book Designer: Staci Harpole, Cubic Design
Illustrator: Kate Reed, Tim Manibusan
Production Assistant: Tim Manibusan
Photography: All flat quilt photographs by Sharon Risedorph. All fabric and how-to photographs by C&T staff.
Published by C&T Publishing, Inc., P.O. Box 1456, Lafayette, California, 94549

Front cover: Detail from *Night Flight* by Linda Potter
Back cover: *Let the Sun Shine In* and *Evening Lilies* by Linda Potter

Library of Congress Cataloging-in-Publication Data

Potter, Linda.
  Quilt & embellish in one step! / Linda Potter.
      p. cm.
  Includes bibliographical references and index.
  ISBN 1-57120-258-7 (paper trade)
  1. Patchwork—Patterns. 2. Quilting—Patterns. 3. Appliqué—Patterns. 4. Embroidery—Patterns. I. Title: Quilt and embellish in one step!. II. Title.

  TT835.P678 2004
  746.46—dc22

                                    2004006137

Printed in China
10 9 8 7 6 5 4 3 2 1

To Ken, with love

Acknowledgments

My appreciation to the many individuals who played a role in the development and publication of Quilt & Embellish in One Step!

▓ The talented staff at C&T Publishing, especially Amy Marson, Gailen Runge, Jan Grigsby, and Gael Betts, for their inspiration, support, and vision in the early stages of the project, and Diane Pedersen, Sara Kate MacFarland, Dave Nash, and Tim Manibusan for their attention to numerous technical details as the project proceeded.

▓ Candie Frankel, my developmental editor, and Staci Harpole, Cubic Design, for their talent and skill in bringing text and visuals together.

▓ Guild members and fellow quilters who have inspired and taught me over the years. I am especially indebted to the Western Michigan Quilt Guild and the Tulip Patchers, who fostered my love of traditional quiltmaking, and the Austin Area Quilt Guild, the Easy Piecers, the Quilted Hearts, and my friend and mentor, Kathleen McCrady, for exposing me to myriad quilting techniques I never would have discovered on my own.

▓ Quilting Creations International, Inc., The Stencil Company, and StenSource International Inc., for quilt stencil designs that continue to inspire me and fill me with ideas.

▓ Quilt artists Mary Mashuta, for the inspirational comments in her book *Wearable Art for Real People*, and Sharon Rexroad, for giving me the final push I needed to begin this endeavor.

▓ Carol Kirchhoff, the owner of Prairie Point, for allowing me to continue my dream, and the staff and students at Prairie Point, who supported and encouraged me all the way.

▓ My dear friends and fellow quilters Leanne Baraban, Charlotte Gurwell, and Judy Oberkrom, who contributed quilts and gave me emotional support through all phases of the project, and for all the contributors whose quilts appear in these pages—Connie Coffman, Kathy Delaney, Nancy Dietz, Barb Fife, Karen Hansen, Jan Keller, Carol Kirchhoff, Dorothy Larsen, Kathy Marolf, Ilyse Moore, Kim Morrow, Jeanne Poore, and Trish Spencer.

▓ My mother, Kay, and my grandmothers, Mable and Myrtle, whose love of the needle arts continues to inspire me.

▓ My father, Jack, and my grandfathers, Adis and Wilder, for encouraging me to always follow my dreams.

▓ Our son, Shawn, for his ability to shed humor on any quilting predicament I get myself into.

▓ And, finally and especially, my dear husband Ken, for his love, support, and encouragement over the years. He makes it possible for me to participate in my dream.

Contents

Introduction

In 1981, after a twenty-year quest to try every form of needlework known to woman, I began a wonderful journey into the world of quiltmaking. It wasn't long before I fell in love with fine hand quilting. I found the rhythmic motion of the needle relaxing and therapeutic. No matter what daily stresses I was experiencing, hand quilting eased me into an almost Zen-like meditation. In the early 1980s, I attended workshops and completed quilts in a variety of styles, the common thread being that all were heavily hand-quilted.

The introduction of rotary cutting equipment, the increased availability of beautifully patterned cotton fabrics, and my purchase of a brand-new sewing machine propelled my quiltmaking skills to a new level. I loved designing quilts and selecting fabrics, and with my new equipment, I was able to turn out more quilt tops at a faster rate. My inability to hand quilt fast enough to keep up with my piecing output proved frustrating. I convinced myself that quilting by machine was the answer, but after trial and error, I concluded that machine quilting was not right for me. In 1994, a job relocation forced me to set my stitching dilemma aside and focus on other areas of my life. During this sabbatical from quilting, an idea started percolating in my mind.

For many years I had admired the Japanese art of *sashiko*. I was especially taken with the images in a beautiful book entitled *Sashiko Blue and White Quilt Art of Japan,* by Kazuko Mende and Reiko Morishige. *Sashiko* is created by working a series of crisp white running stitches on a single layer of indigo fabric. In ancient Japan, peasants used *sashiko* to reinforce very thin fabrics; unlike quilting, there is no batting or backing. The thicker thread used for *sashiko* stitching reminded me of the embroidery floss I had used as a child and also of the decorative stitches used to embellish crazy quilts. Then I came across an intriguing section in Mary Mashuta's *Wearable Art for Real People* describing the use of perle cotton to quilt clothing. Thoughts about these various techniques mingled in my mind. Why not put them all together while I am quilting? It was in this way that my idea for creative quilted embellishment was born. I call it Needle Magic.

My immediate goal was to develop a hand-quilting technique that would allow me to finish quilts more quickly. I endeavored to re-create the visual impact of *sashiko* on pieced and appliquéd quilts using a variety of colored threads. As my experimenting progressed, I began incorporating more of the decorative embroidered embellishment associated with crazy quilting. This decorative stitching brought dimension and texture to the quilt surface. Appliqué and beading soon followed, adding a final touch.

Quilt & Embellish in One Step! is my way of sharing my Needle Magic embellishment repertoire with you and helping you make it your own. You can use this approach to finish quilt tops you have made and set aside or to design brand-new quilts. I hope it will help you rediscover— or discover anew—the Zen of hand quilting.

The book's opening chapters contain design insights and recommendations for fabrics, tools, and supplies. Next come step-by-step instructions for the various stitching, appliqué, and beading techniques I use. Four project quilts demonstrate how these techniques can be incorporated into different quilt-making styles. But please don't stop there. As the many gallery quilts illustrate, the unique zest of Needle Magic can be applied to quilts of all design persuasions.

Let the magic begin!

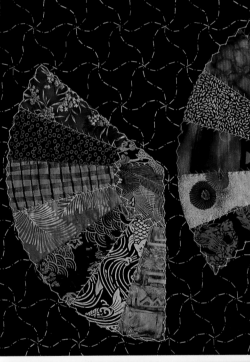

Sashiko-style quilting fills the background around appliquéd and embellished fans. Detail from *Japanese Fans* by Barbara Fife.

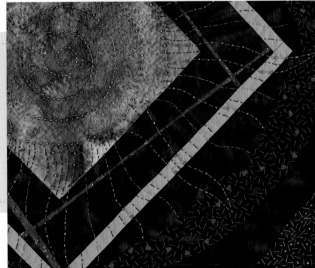

The artist used seed-stitch embellishment, hand-painted fabric, and beading to enhance her quilt. Detail from Charlotte Gurwell's *Citron Explosion.*

The Art
of Embellishment

Throughout my two-decade quilting career, I have been exposed to many different types and styles of quilts and fabrics. My earliest interests focused on the richness of traditional quilts. My membership in the Austin Area Quilt Guild in Texas gave me privileged access to award-winning quilts, ranging from beautiful reproduction quilts, made by my friend and mentor, Kathleen McCrady, to the quilts of contemporary quiltmaker-artists. A move to Overland Park, Kansas, brought me in contact with comforting primitive-style quilts as well as antique quilts. My experience working in a quilt shop, planning classes, and assisting students and customers has given me even more styles, patterns, and techniques to choose from. Through all of my quilting explorations and detours, one factor has emerged a constant:

" I love hand quilting.
I can spot it a mile away.
My heart races with passion whenever I see it. "

Quilting by Hand

Detail from Linda Potter's *Whig Rose II*.

Garden Oasis, Leanne M. Baraban, 2003, 52" x 23". Hand-dyed cotton fabrics, #8 perle cotton, beads, batting. Machine-pieced, hand-quilted, beaded. This quilt won the viewers' choice award at the Kaw Valley Quilt Guild Show 2003 in Lawrence, Kansas. The embellishment stitching on this wholecloth quilt is based on a copyright-free design from the book *Floral Ornament* by Carol Belanger Grafton (Dover, 1977).

Hand quilting attracts me in several ways. First, there's the sculptural beauty. Hand stitching creates tiny hills and valleys across the surface of the quilt that invite touching. Machine quilting can mimic, but never entirely capture, this characteristic beauty. Emotionally, there's a sense of history and personal associations. You can't help but wonder what hidden dramas were unfolding in the life of the quilter as she plied her needle. Then, there's the "coffee break" angle. When I am stitching, I can relax, unwind, and let go of built-up tensions. Quilting helps me feel calm, yet simultaneously energized and productive. I value hand quilting because I like the way it looks and because it has such a good effect on me. As I pushed forward with new techniques, I wanted to retain the aspects of hand quilting that I valued. I had already begun to see how thread

colors and textures could enliven a quilt. Basically, I wanted to capture the aesthetic impact and personal pleasures of hand quilting while shortening the time commitment required to achieve them.

Design Sources

Needle Magic is a design-driven art. The designs you quilt are bold embroideries, done in thick threads, and done in color. The quilted designs become an integral part of the quilt. They can be used to convey a sense of physical motion, to create a pictorial scene, or to set a mood. They should not be construed as an afterthought or as an accent. This is not to say you cannot use the technique on a quilt top you have already designed and completed. But the more rewarding path is to design a quilt with an embellishment strategy already in mind.

Designs can come from many sources. Pattern books with copyright-free or personal use patterns are widely available. Don't limit yourself to quilting books. Designs for crafts such as stained glass, ironwork, wood carving, and embroidery can give you fresh interpretations of a variety of motifs. Free-motion machine quilting patterns can look beautiful when rendered by hand. Photography books offer close-up views of quilts and other textiles that you might not otherwise get to see. Soon after I began quilting, photographs of antique quilts inspired me to try stippling and feathers

with fine hand quilting. To this day, I use feathers in quilts whenever I get a chance.

I advise my students to keep a file of quilting designs they find inspiring. You might include photos taken at quilt shows (when the venue permits photography), photocopies of quilts from books that you own, gallery and exhibit handouts, or clippings from magazines and newspapers. Most quiltmakers own an impressive library of quilting books and sources, but few take the time to collect the best ideas in one place.

Another design source I frequently tap is my collection of quilting stencils. Quiltmakers tend to have an endless supply of fabrics, but they neglect their stencil collections. If you are a hand quilter, or want to become one, and are reluctant to draw your own designs, you need to collect stencils to assist you. Even though I try to consciously choose my quilting designs at the start of a project, sometimes things don't work out as I have planned and I must search for an idea after the quilt top is completed. Stencils have come to my rescue more than once.

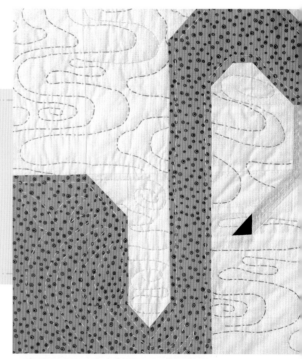

Dark on light. Deep blue quilting turns a white background fabric into a watery lagoon. Detail from *Funky Flamingos* by Kathy Marolf. Original Marilyn Dorwart pattern.

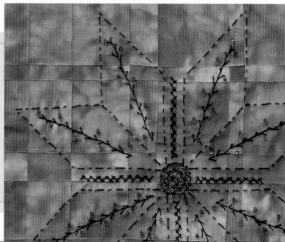

Dark on brights. A star quilted in strong, dark thread overlays colorful fabrics. Detail from *Blaubeuren* by Nancy Dietz, using the Ricky Tims pattern Harmonic Convergence.

As a quilter, you probably already see designs for patchwork or appliqué in your head. Now you need to take that imaginative power one step further. Conjure up images of stitches and form them into designs. Mentally fuse your embellishment concepts onto your quilt plan. Think big. Let all the elements interconnect. Record your ideas by writing, sketching, making a design board, or any other way that works for you.

Colors That Work

There are many exciting visual effects you can achieve when you quilt with perle cotton. Thread colors that are unexpected or offbeat are the norm rather than the exception for me. Playing with different thread and fabric color combinations is an exercise I never tire of. Here are some ideas to consider.

Pull out the stops. Wild thread and fabric colors rev up a simple two-block patchwork. Detail from *Heart Blossoms* by Kim Morrow, using a Linda Potter pattern.

Use "wrong" colors. Yellow and pink are not the first colors one usually thinks of for leaves. Here, yellow and pink quilting echoes the layered effect of the green leaf appliqués. Detail from Dorothy Larsen's *Moon Glow*.

Values that match. Medium-value green thread adds visible texture to a rose-colored border, without overpowering the delicate floral print. Peach threads quilted against a paler cream-colored background are less noticeable, for a more subtle texture around a quilted butterfly. Detail from Linda Potter's *Serenity*.

Camouflage. Highly patterned fabrics tend to swallow up the embellishment work entirely—an effect that is not usually desirable, but perfect for this crazy quilt application. Detail from Linda Potter's *Delightfully Victorian*.

Light on dark. A variegated thread ranging from off-white to orange brightens a dark solid border. The result is a beautiful luminous effect. Detail from Barb Fife's *Japanese Fans*.

Color swapping. Autumnal hues pass back and forth freely between fabrics and threads in this visual cornucopia. The quiltmaker used a design by Ruth Powers for Innovations Patterns. She added Linda Potter's embellishment technique for the leaf veins. Detail from *Third Weekend in October* by Janet Keller.

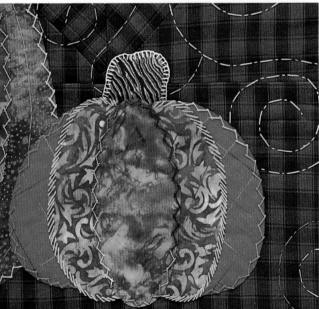

Hue intensity. Neon-like thread colors accentuate the rind and stem of an appliquéd pumpkin. Detail from Linda Potter's *Pumpkin Party*.

Hidden Benefits

In addition to being beautiful to look at, Needle Magic has its "secret" benefits. It lets you:

■ **Enjoy the process.** Not everyone has the time, inclination, or patience to pursue fine hand quilting. Needle Magic brings the art—and the Zen—of hand quilting to a larger audience.

■ **Quilt without pain.** Needle Magic seems to put less stress on the hands than traditional hand quilting. If you suffer from the onset of arthritis or carpal tunnel syndrome, Needle Magic may be a technique that you can continue to do.

■ **Quilt without guilt.** Using larger stitches on purpose takes you out of the "my stitches are too big" guilt trip. Who needs psychological stress when doing something for fun?

■ **Quilt with flexibility.** A varying stitch length lets you avoid bulky junctures at the seams without ruining the symmetry.

■ **Indulge your senses.** It's exciting and stimulating to work with beautifully colored threads and gorgeous fabrics and beads. You'll exercise your mind as well as your eyes and hands.

■ **Achieve dynamic results quickly.** You don't have to embellish the entire quilt. Save time by machine quilting most of the surface and then adding hand-quilted embellishment in selected areas.

Yellow quilting stitches embellish selected blocks of a machine-quilted piece. Detail from Linda Potter's *Fractured Snowballs*.

Supplies

My experiments with various supplies have evolved over time. I started out by trying embroidery floss and perle cotton #5 on my quilt Jazzy Mountains. Although the results were visually pleasing, the actual quilting experience proved somewhat frustrating. Four strands of embroidery floss refused to stay together neatly. Regardless of the care I took at the beginning to separate them from the skein, I ended up with loops and knots. Perle cotton #5 made a strong visual statement in the border, but I found the thread thickness difficult to needle through the fabric and batting. My overriding goal was to maintain stitching ease and enjoyment while still adding dimension and texture to the quilt surface. Over time, I discovered the right combination of thread, batting, needle, and other supplies to pull it all together.

Jazzy Mountains

by Linda Potter, 1995, 52" x 68"

Cotton fabrics, #5 perle cotton, embroidery floss, Thermore batting. Machine-pieced, hand-quilted. From a design by Nancy Brennan Daniel in her book *Delectable Mountain Quilts: A New View* (American School of Needlework, 1993).

Linda's first quilt using her Needle Magic techniques. The quilt received third place in the innovative category at the IQA Quilt Show in 1995.

Perle Cotton

Perle cotton is a tightly twisted two-ply thread. It is produced in five sizes (#3, #5, #8, #12, and #16) for various types of embroidery. Because the twist of the thread remains constant during stitching, perle cotton makes a more suitable medium for quilting than embroidery floss. The smooth cotton fiber easily needles through both fabric and batting.

I tried #5 perle cotton first, but soon switched to #8, which is slightly thinner and easier to thread, yet still thick enough to make a pleasing visual impact. I do sometimes still use #5 when I want to create an exceptionally strong visual effect. In areas calling for a higher density of quilting or smaller stitches, you can go even thinner, to #12.

#8 Perle Cotton

Quality counts when it comes to thread. As you try different brands, look for two features:

■ Long staple cotton fibers— Choose the type of thread normally used for fine embroidery on linen. Long staple cotton fibers are better able to withstand the process of being repeatedly dragged through the fabric and batting as the stitches are formed.

■ Solid-dyed colors—The advantage of solid dying is that the thread is colorfast. The colors will not fade or run.

A key attraction of perle cotton is the gorgeous and extensive color selection. In ordinary fine hand quilting, the color of the quilting thread tends to have little or no effect on the general appearance of the quilt. With embellishment quilting, the whole idea is to make the thread visible. For more on choosing thread colors, see page 23.

As you shop, you are bound to come across beautiful decorative yarns and threads geared to the needlepoint, knitting, and crochet markets or manufactured for machine bobbin drawing. Most of these products are not suitable for Needle Magic. They are too textured and coarse and not sturdy enough to withstand the heavy stress of stitching. But you *can* use them for wrapping and lacing techniques.

Fabric and Batting

The fabric and batting—the layers that you stitch through—can make or break your embellishment quilting experience. I prefer working with high-quality, 100% cotton fabrics—the fabrics you'd normally use for quiltmaking. Yes, you can use tightly woven batiks; just avoid them when you are first starting out, as the high thread count makes the needling more difficult.

Batting plays a critical supporting role. In traditional hand and machine quilting, the stitching "sculpts" the surface of the quilt. In embellishment work, the sandwiched layers are pulled less tightly. Interest is created by the color and pattern of the stitches, not by contrast between padded and compressed areas. An appropriate batting will be thin enough to allow your decorative stitches to sit on the surface of the quilt sandwich. If the loft is too high and the stitches sink down into ditches and valleys, the effect will be lost. I occasionally use very thin cotton batting for embellishment techniques, but the product I most prefer is Thermore by Hobbs. Originally designed for quilted clothing, it is sold in queen-size packages and by the yard. Thermore batting is thin and lightweight, with a low loft. It is easy to quilt with thicker threads and larger needles. The batting fibers will not migrate, shift, or beard, and the characteristic sticky quality encourages the fabric and batting to cling to each other, even in areas with minimal or no quilting.

Tools of the Trade

This section discusses the special tools you will need to work the combination embellishment and quilting stitches I teach in this book. All of the project quilts (pages 58–77) require the tools described here.

Widely spaced quilting lines represent gusts of wind. Detail from Karen Hansen's *Falling Leaves*.

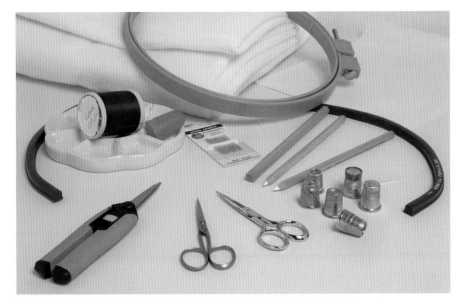

Tools for Needle Magic

Stencils can be used separately or in combination with other designs to embellish a quilt. Designs from different manufacturers can be brought together on the same quilt. For the most satisfactory results, choose designs that are open and flowing to accommodate the larger stitches.

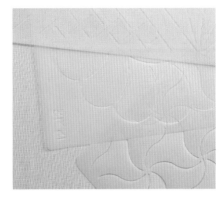

Quilting Stencils

Crewel/Embroidery Needles

In my first attempts at embellishment quilting, I used quilting betweens several sizes larger than those I used for fine hand quilting. The larger eye size accommodated thicker threads, but the shaft was fairly thick and hard to needle through the fabric and batting. Betweens are short in length, which is appropriate for fine hand quilting but less desirable for the larger stitches used in embellishment work. I could load only one stitch at a time.

My search for something better led me to crewel/embroidery needles. These needles are longer than betweens and have a narrower shaft. With a size 7 needle, I could easily needle through the fabric and batting and load two to three stitches at a time. The threading was a little difficult because the eye is somewhat small for the thread, but the good needling quality more than made up for it. Try several sizes to determine which works best for you.

Quilting Stencils

Collecting stencils for quilting designs is as important to me as collecting fabric. Quilting stencils come in a large variety of sizes and designs. They are made of heavy-duty plastic and can be reused indefinitely. I've purchased stencils from a variety of sources, including quilt shops and vendors at major quilt shows. Online shopping is also available. My students complain that many quilt shops simply don't carry enough stencils. I think that is because people don't buy enough of them; it's a trend I'd love to see reversed. Some quilters solve the problem by designing and making their own stencils using stencil-cutting and stencil-burning tools.

Marking Tools

Quilt marking is a matter of personal preference. You should choose the tools and approach that work for you. Most of my quilts make use of patterned fabrics and dark or unusual colors. I like to use fabric markers that show up but that also rub off easily. I mark my quilts in stages as I work, rather than all at once at the beginning.

Round Quilting Hoops

When I began my self-taught adventure in fine hand quilting, ignorance led me to work without a hoop. (I thought quilt frames no longer existed.) Quilting a small square was easy, but when I graduated to the sampler quilt I pieced in my first quilt class, "hoopless" quilting was next to impossible. After some initial experimentation, I found a 10" round quilting hoop to be the perfect size for my short arms and small hands. This diameter allowed me to reach easily into the center of the hoop. Soon I was quilting 12 stitches to the inch (measured on the surface of the quilt).

When I moved on to larger projects, I tried larger hoops. I learned, through trial and error, that a 12" round hoop was the correct size for me. Hoops larger than 12" required me to reach farther, causing stress on my wrist, arm, neck, shoulders, and back. To determine your correct hoop size for fine hand quilting, measure from the inside crook of your elbow to your fingertips. The hoop diameter should not exceed this measurement.

When I began embellishment quilting, I continued to use a 12" round quilting hoop. My only complaint was that because the stitches work up so quickly, it seemed as though I was constantly adjusting the hoop position. A 14" hoop gave me a bit more working space without causing physical stress. I think this is because embellishment stitching does not require the same fine motor skills as fine hand quilting. Today, I use all three sizes: 10", 12", and 14".

My favorite hoop type is a plastic nonslip hoop that appeared on the market shortly after I began embellishment quilting. Being the dutiful quilt instructor and consumer that I am, I decided to try this new product. Instead of two flat rings, the newer hoop is grooved where the two rings meet. The groove holds the quilt in the desired position without crushing stitches and beads. The outer edges are more rounded than on traditional hoops, for less abrasion on decorative stitches. (See Resources, page 94.)

Students often ask if square or oval quilt hoops can be used. My advice is no. Needle Magic often necessitates turning the quilt hoop and stitching from many different directions. Only a round hoop is truly comfortable to use.

Quilting Hoop

Thimble

As with any hand-quilting technique, an excellent-quality metal thimble with good dimples is recommended. Thimbles are used to rock the needle during the stitching. I wear my thimble on the middle finger of my writing hand. It is also appropriate to wear a thimble on the index finger of your writing hand or on your thumb, your strongest finger. Choose the thimble size and position that feel comfortable to you.

Rubber Finger

Hand quilting places stress on the writing hand each time it pulls the needle from the fabric. This is especially true with embellishment work, when several stitches are carried on the needle. My secret weapon is a rubber finger, worn on the thumb of my writing hand. Available in office-supply stores, rubber fingers were originally manufactured to give office workers better traction when they were filing paperwork or thumbing through card files or a telephone directory. I wear one to get a better grip on the needle. I prefer a size that is small enough to stay put on my finger but not so tight that my finger becomes overly warm.

Work Environment

Create a work environment that is conducive to creativity as well as productivity. Choose a comfortable chair with good support. Add a table if you plan to do beading work. Most important, be sure to provide ample ambient light as well as direct task lighting.

Designing
Your Quilt

A s any quiltmaker knows, planning a new quilt project is one of the most exciting parts of the quiltmaking process. Nothing beats the thrill of coming up with just the right design and fabrics to unite in the perfect quilt marriage. Unfortunately, the manner and style in which the quilt will be quilted often become an afterthought, something to be considered later.

With Needle Magic, that approach is not an option. The quilting itself is so essential to the design, you have to consider it up front, right along with your fabric and color palette. Not every quilt is a good candidate for Needle Magic. If you are going to spend precious time quilting by hand, you must do more than choose a design that you love. You must also seek out designs that will receive the maximum enhancement from the embellishments that you add.

The Four Factors

There are four distinct factors that contribute to a successfully embellished quilt design. Let's begin by looking at each factor individually.

Factor #1: *Quilt Pattern*

The quilt pattern refers to the design made by the patchwork or appliquéd shapes. To focus on the quilt pattern, picture a quilt top without any quilting. Now remove all the color from your mental picture, so that the only thing remaining are the seamlines. This is the quilt pattern.

Appliqué quilts with plain background space around or between the motifs is another option.

60-Degree Sampler Quilt

60-Degree Sampler Quilt Pattern

One option for embellishment work is to choose a quilt pattern with open areas in the background. Open areas give you a space to show off unique quilting. Examples include quilts with wide, plain borders, diagonally set quilts with open blocks, and medallion quilts that feature large open areas around a central motif.

Stylized carrots are quilted in the open spaces around four rabbit appliqués. The rabbits wear dimensional embroidered vests that represent the four seasons. Detail from *Rabbit Run*, a table runner by Ilyse Moore.

Patchwork quilt patterns are another option. Here, you can add decorative stitching between the blocks and borders or along other seamlines to accentuate selected patchwork shapes. Be sure to choose patchwork patterns with large, well-defined shapes. Avoid patterns with lots of small, intricate pieces—they are interesting enough on their own without the added embellishment, and besides, you wouldn't want to stitch through the extra fabric thickness. In *Elegant Embellishments,* I used deep burgundy stitching to define the inner border strips and distinguish them from the low-contrast background. Yellow stitching accomplishes a similar purpose for the patchwork stars in *Night Flight.*

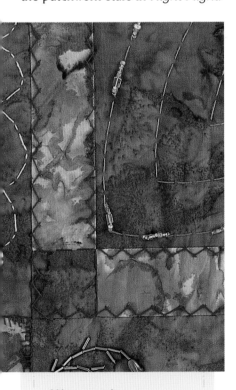

Vibrant perle cotton quilting visibly separates fabrics with low contrast. Detail from Linda Potter's *Elegant Embellishments.*

Factor #2: *Quilting Design*

The quilting design is the actual pattern that the quilting stitches trace on the surface of the quilt. To focus on the quilting design, visualize the quilt top without any seamlines or color.

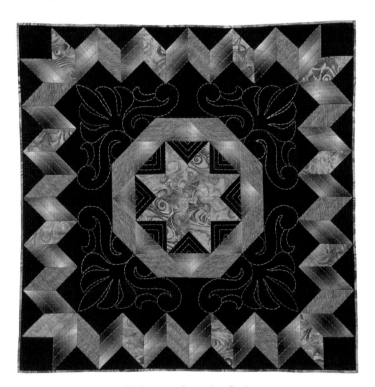

60-Degree Sampler Quilt

60-Degree Sampler Quilting Design

In a well-executed design, the style or theme of the quilting relates to the overall theme of the quilt. As I mentioned, I take most of my quilting designs from purchased stencils and have built an extensive collection of stencils over the years. In the early planning stages of your quilt, lay out the stencils that are possible candidates and see how you might work them into your design. For *Nagano '98,* a Japanese-inspired quilt, I drew upon my collection of *sashiko* stencils. In *Serenity,* I quilted butterflies around an appliquéd floral medallion. Designs can also come from a printed fabric, patchwork shapes, or appliqués.

Quilting designs that are open and flowing, rather than tight and intricate, are ideal for embellishment work. Part of the reason is the thicker weight of perle cotton and the appearance it makes on the quilt. Stitching lines that crowd together can appear dense, heavy, and clumsy. Remember, in perle cotton stitching, a little design goes a long way.

Of course, the quilting design must be the appropriate size and shape for the allotted space. The design you choose to fill a plain block will be different from the design used in a border. Here you can begin to see how Factor #1 and Factor #2 must be considered in tandem.

One way to think about the four factors is to divide them into two groups:

■ *Black-and-white.* Factors #1 and #2 belong to this group. With just pencil and paper, you can sketch different versions of your quilt and think about the design without any color issues to distract you.

■ *Color.* Factors #3 and #4 belong to this group. Here's where you get to introduce color options, select your fabrics, and audition those glorious thread colors.

Factor #3: Fabric

In any quilt, fabrics play a starring role. Like quilting designs, fabric patterns can be keyed to the overall theme of the quilt. In order to select a fabric palette, the quiltmaker evaluates how different fabrics "behave" when placed alongside one another. Quiltmakers use contrasts in color, value, visual texture, and scale to bring patchwork and appliqué patterns to life.

With Needle Magic, all the usual rules of fabric selection apply, with one addition: You have to remember that certain fabrics will become the background for the decorative stitching. At first glance, it might seem as though only fabrics with little or no pattern are suitable. But in fact, Needle Magic lets you select and use some highly patterned fabrics. The many blue and blue-green background fabrics in *Night Flight* were chosen for their lively patterns and subtle color variations. The only caveat was that each fabric provide a contrasting backdrop for the particular perle cotton colors placed against it. The overall palette is simple, but the color interplay is rich and complex.

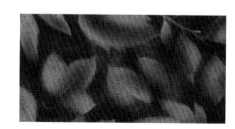

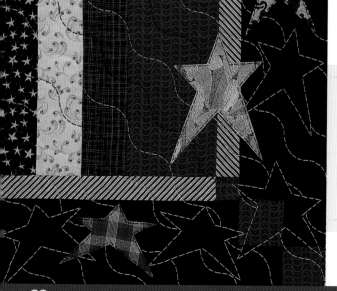

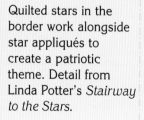

Quilted stars in the border work alongside star appliqués to create a patriotic theme. Detail from Linda Potter's *Stairway to the Stars.*

Factor #4: Thread

Thread color is the final element to consider in your quilt design. Be prepared to throw out your preconceived ideas about which color threads look right against which fabrics. The world of Needle Magic is full of color surprises, and the more daring you are, the more dynamic your quilts will become. Extreme color contrasts are often necessary to ensure the visibility of the thread. Instead of a toned-down burgundy, for example, try bright red. For greens, try lime or chartreuse; for rust shades, try bright orange; for gold, try bright yellow. *Pumpkin Party* (page 90) gets its kick from the yellow, orange, and lime green stitching. In *Through the Garden Window* (detail on page 24), I quilted red thread against a lavender fabric. This clashing color combination unleashes its own magic. The red stitching softens the lavender and gives it the look and feel of a print. This, in turn, helps the lavender fabric blend more harmoniously with the quilt's theme print.

The *Night Flight* Fabric Palette

In addition to planning the quilt top, there's the fun of selecting fabric for the back. Needle Magic tends to produce a variety of unusual and prominent stitches on the back of the quilt. To camouflage these stitches, I invariably choose a highly patterned fabric for the backing.

Red stitching on lavender fabric helps all the quilt fabrics harmonize. Detail from Linda Potter's *Through the Garden Window.*

Push yourself to go beyond the obvious color choice whenever possible. Ecru thread was a natural for *Fractured Snowballs* (from page 84)—it just wasn't terribly exciting. Yellow thread gave me the same value contrast, picked up the gold metallic highlights in some of the fabrics, and looked more dynamic against the reds. In fact, one of the thread colors I encourage students to audition is yellow. On many fabrics, but especially darker fabrics, yellow stitching creates little rays of sunshine that give the quilt a unique, luminous quality. It doesn't seem to matter which shade of yellow is used.

Another color that adapts well is dark forest green. Both yellow-based and blue-based shades of forest green blend well together. On some backgrounds, they even look like the same color. One shade can easily be substituted for the other, should you run out.

To audition a thread color, lay a strand of the thread across the background fabric. Cover the spool or skein so that the concentration of color does not divert your eye. Viewing a single strand will give you a better idea of how the thread color will actually look on the surface of the quilt. Stand back several feet to see how the thread color interacts with the fabrics. Try to visualize even less of the thread color, to account for the portions that will sink into the batting or fall on the back of the quilt. If you are uncertain about the color proportions, thread a needle and run a series of stitches through the fabric.

Keep an open mind as you perform this simple color exercise.

Remember, many color combinations that seem inappropriate will visually blend in a totally harmonious way. Unexpected or extreme color combinations are the norm in successful embellishment work, but you do have to train your eye to recognize and appreciate them. Don't shrink back from experimentation. When you are stitching, use variations on a single color, like the dark greens I mentioned earlier. In spite of the huge thread palette available, there will never be enough thread colors—quilters will always want more! Build a lively thread stash, and don't be afraid to make substitutions. When you run out of one color, pick up another, and don't worry if it is a slightly different shade.

Sometimes, no matter how hard you try, no thread choice will seem right. Usually, it's a problem of a poor fabric/thread coordination or the lack of overall planning from the beginning. I learned not to force the issue when I tried to find thread colors for a pastel print quilt top I had already made. I auditioned yellow, purple, and teal perle cotton, but it soon became clear that against the busy prints only the purple would show up. The lighter colors would "disappear." If I had gone ahead and used the purple thread to outline or quilt in-the-ditch, I would have ruined my vision of softly mingling prints. Rather than spend time on hand quilting that wouldn't show, I asked my friend Kelly Ashton to machine-quilt it for me.

Three Approaches

In a successfully embellished quilt design, the four factors—quilt pattern, quilting design, fabric, and thread—combine into a harmonious and unified whole. You can approach the design process any number of ways.

In a straightforward, methodical approach, you'd start with the quilt pattern, choose quilting designs, and then pick out your fabrics and threads. Even though you might have an overall idea of the quilt in your mind from the beginning, you tackle the design process step by step. This neat, orderly approach is safe, but it's not for everyone.

I often work backward, starting with a quilting design that I want to use and then searching for a pattern to show it off. Or perhaps I've found a beautiful piece of fabric that would be perfect for Needle Magic (the sign of a true fabric addict) and can't wait to find quilting designs and threads to go with it. Creative people tend to break out beyond the constraints of linear thinking in all sorts of ways. They like to think about lots of different factors at the same time and actually thrive on the mental stimulation.

The approaches I give here chronicle the creation of three quilts. Put together, they will give you an idea of some of the ways a quilt design can come together. As you will see, creative work rarely follows a set course.

Approach #1: *Turtle Heaven*

Turtle Heaven demonstrates what I call the "gradual simultaneous" execution of a quilt design. Here, I expanded on an idea for a fan quilt. The various design elements occurred to me slowly and in stages, resulting in a theme that permeates the entire quilt.

Not all quilts are "ripe" for embellishment. These busy prints looked great on their own, and the author decided not to tamper with them.

What to Avoid

■ Lots of busy, highly patterned fabrics

■ Tiny, intricate patchwork or appliqué

■ Dense patchwork with no open spaces for quilting

Before Quilting

After Quilting

Turtle Heaven

by Linda Potter, 2003,
43 ½" x 62 ½"

Cotton fabrics, #8 perle
cotton, Thermore batting.
Machine-pieced, hand-
appliquéd, hand-quilted.

I had been playing with various designs for fan quilts on the computer when I came up with an unusual setting of red fans on a purple background. I began a fabric search in my stash, and in among the ever-growing stacks, I came across a fun tropical print. It showed fish and sea coral in shades of pink, coral, and red against a purple background. This fabric gave me an idea for a vast underwater scene. The red fans would become a coral reef.

As I browsed through various media for underwater pictures, I came across several photos of green sea turtles. These photos reminded me of turtles we had once seen on a day sailing trip around the Napali Coast of Kauai, Hawaii. I began visualizing water currents and seaweed, which I could depict with various shades of blue, yellow, and green thread. There could be a mother turtle swimming toward the surface with other smaller turtles around her.

Perhaps I would add fish. By combining piecework, fabrics, and decorative quilting, I had conjured up a "turtle heaven."

The final problem I had to resolve concerned the borders. The left and bottom borders had become part of my underwater scene. At the top and right, I had chosen bright border strips to mark the top and side edges of an aquarium. These strong yellow lines contain my underwater world and give the viewer a unique cross section of it. Bright yellow threads of sunshine beam down on the water and illumine the aquarium edge. You can almost feel the warmth of the penetrating light.

Green seaweed is worked in straight running stitches and then wrapped with two strands of yellow perle cotton.

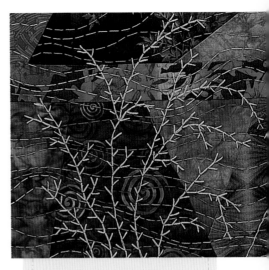

Seaweed depicted with the Magic Fern stitch—two colors of thread—yellow and green—are stitched at one time using a special needle with two eyes.

Layers of stitching in different colors create gentle underwater undulation. The trailing coral stems are made by wrapping pink thread around red running stitches. Each twiggy growth spur is a cluster of five straight stitches.

Sun rays are made by wrapping straight stitches with a single strand of perle cotton.

A thread "painting" technique creates water currents around a mother turtle.

Approach #2: *Night Flight*

Night Flight is a fabric-driven quilt. The fabrics I selected were medium to dark prints with subtle color variations, making them perfect backgrounds for embellishment. I assembled two vibrant color groups—one with blue-greens (see page 23) and the other with yellow-greens. The darker fabrics would allow me to quilt highly visible designs using yellow thread.

Night Flight

by Linda Potter, 2003, 54 1/2" x 39 1/2"

Cotton fabrics, #8 perle cotton, Thermore batting. Machine-pieced, hand-quilted, beaded. For full view of quilt, see page 75.

With my fabrics in hand, I set about designing a quilt on the computer. I knew I wanted to use the blue-greens for the background. Against that background would go yellow-green somethings—but what? Of the several possibilities that popped into my head, my hands-down favorite was stars. Here, then, was my underlying design plan: a night-time scene with stars.

Next, I considered what and where to quilt. I could, of course, quilt more stars, but that would be obvious and *too* simple. I am constitutionally disinclined to make anything too simple. As I looked over my stencil collection, a butterfly and cattail stencil caught my eye. My imagination moved swiftly, carrying me to a vision of butterflies dancing above and around cattails at the water's edge.

To begin the thread selection process, I laid the fabrics on a table, folding and overlapping them to represent a scenario similar in shape and size to the quilt I was envisioning. Then I began laying strands of various threads on the fabric to determine which colors would be the most visible. I chose bright yellow for the stars and light green for the grasses. For the water—a challenge, given the blue-green background fabric—I decided on light blue. For the butterflies, I moved to pink, lavender, and orange threads and beads. The orange thread and beads provided a sharp contrast to the background, while pink and lavender threads and beads reward viewers who move in for a closer look.

Adding beads as you quilt is a fun activity and lends a serendipitous quality to the quilt.

If you are new to Needle Magic, you may be tempted to postpone the thread selection until after the quilt top is completed. Resist this urge. Selecting the quilting threads before you start piecing gives you a decided advantage. It ensures that the total quilt picture will feature sufficient fabric/thread contrast. Remember, in Needle Magic, the quilt is not just the fabrics. The fabrics plus the stitching make the design, and the colors of both must work together to carry off the design impact you intend. Swapping fabric colors in and out of the design is easy in the planning stages but becomes much harder after the sewing commences.

Another advantage to early thread selection is the motivation factor. I am always eager to hand quilt. Having all the thread colors picked out and ready to go helps me move through the piecing phase faster to get to my reward.

Quilting stitches impart a quiet, humming energy to the patchwork surface. In this nighttime pond scene, you can almost hear the crickets chirping.

Approach #3:
60-Degree Sampler

The *60-Degree Sampler* is aptly named, for this quilt truly does showcase a variety of supplies, techniques, and fabrics that I had been itching to use. A driving force behind the quilt design is the large corner scroll design, available to me on a quilt stencil I owned. I had yet to find a quilt pattern where I could show off these graciously curving lines to good effect. I was also longing to experiment with some designer #5 perle cotton manufactured by The Caron Collection. The quilting stencil and thread were making a tenuous connection in my mind, but my vision for a full quilt was not yet complete.

Around this time, I became intrigued with 60° triangles and piecing angles and the 3-D illusions they could create. I had never tackled 60° angles before, and I looked forward to the challenge. I decided on a star bordered with 60° triangles for the center of the quilt. Once I had this much figured out, I began looking through my stash for appropriate fabrics. Because it was important for the quilted scrollwork to be visible on the background, I started there, auditioning various shades of thread on my different fabrics. I settled on a light variegated thread for the stitching and dark navy batik for the background. Then I began a search for more fabrics to carry off the 3-D illusion. A large-scale homespun plaid in shades of blue worked particularly well with the navy batik. I rounded out the fabric

60-Degree Sampler

by Linda Potter, 1998, 37" x 37"
Cotton fabrics, The Caron Collection variegated thread #5 and #8 perle cotton, Thermore batting. Machine-pieced, hand-quilted.

palette with a chartreuse batik and another shade of green batik.

The final quilt design came about primarily through trial and error. I began with an eight-pointed star surrounded by 60° triangles, as planned. After a little measuring and manipulating on the design wall, I found that if I placed the design on point, the quilted scrolls would fit nicely in the setting triangles. From there, I progressed to the border and more trial-and-error piecing. Eventually, I discovered a way to fit the star and quilted scrolls inside the pieced border.

A common guideline in quilt design is to pair curving quilting lines with geometric patchwork and straight quilting lines with curved piecing

or appliqué. Although I often bend these guidelines, this principle was certainly at work in *60-Degree Sampler*. The quilted corner scrolls are beautifully complementary to the patchwork, thanks to the color contrast and The Caron Collection thread. This thicker-weight thread is a challenge to quilt with but results in a splendid graphic line, especially when variegated colors are used. Quilting on the pieced sections was completed with bright yellow #8 perle cotton.

Quilting
Stitches

Since 1995, one of my greatest joys has been teaching beginning quiltmaking classes. I love seeing the eyes of first-time quilters light up when they complete their first four-patch, move from simple to more complex blocks, and complete their first quilt top. I always begin each class with lessons in hand quilting, and I encourage my students to discover the pleasure of hand quilting for themselves.

In listening to various friends, students, and nationally known quilt artists, both in person and on television, I have become aware that I am not alone in my exuberant, passionate love of hand quilting. As fulfilling as it is to own a quilt quilted by hand, I find that what I enjoy even more is the **doing**. Quilting by hand totally absorbs me as nothing else does. Like many hand quilters, I crave the process itself and treasure any time I can set aside for this relaxing and rewarding endeavor. The gentle, rhythmic motion of the needle as it enters the fabric, glides through the batting layer, disappears under the quilt, and emerges once again on the surface is calming and mesmerizing. I call this effect The Zen of Hand Quilting.

As much as I love traditional fine hand quilting, I concede that not everyone gets as excited about tiny, evenly spaced stitches as I do. Needle Magic lets quilters of all abilities and stitching persuasions try their hand and achieve success. In fact, beginning quilters sometimes fare better than more experienced hand quilters, who must force themselves to loosen up and stitch bigger. Larger, irregular stitches are actually a plus because they add such lively texture and surface interest to the quilt.

In this chapter, you'll learn how to work eight Needle Magic stitches. Some of the stitches you will recognize as traditional embroidery stitches adapted to quilting. Keep in mind that the exact stitch length and formation is up to you. As in any other quilting technique, the more you practice, the more needle control you'll obtain. Not every quilter will attain uniform stitches, even with practice, and that is okay. I won't be sending any real or imaginary quilting police to peer over your shoulder. My goal is to make hand quilting accessible,

not frustrate you with rules that take the joy out of stitching. Define your own goals and work toward them.

A minor drawback of using embroidery-style stitches to perform a quilting function is the creation of unorthodox stitches on the back of the quilt. I've made an effort to adapt the stitches for an appealing quilt back. If your quilts must pass the scrutiny of a judge's eye, you may wish to alter your stitching path to conform to the rules of the show. If you are quilting for yourself, your family, or your friends, you need please only yourself. Using a highly patterned fabric for the back of the quilt helps to camouflage the stitches.

Hand Quilting Basics

This section explains the basics of hand quilting, as I have adapted them for the Needle Magic technique. No matter which stitches you choose, the preliminaries are the same. Be sure to hand baste your quilt; safety pins will not work with a quilt hoop and the embellishment stitches may catch on them. You'll need to secure the layered and basted quilt in a hoop, thread the needle, practice a comfortable hand motion, and know how to start and end. If you already practice fine hand quilting, many of these techniques will come easily to you. If you are trying hand quilting for the first time, you'll have the opportunity to develop good habits from the start.

Colorful Needle Magic quilting. Detail from Linda Potter's *The Splendid Poppy*.

Using a Hoop

Be sure to select a comfortable hoop size (see pages 17–18). Experiment with various degrees of tautness. Some quilters prefer their quilt loose for traditional fine hand quilting. Needle Magic uses techniques similar to embroidery. In my experience, it is easier to perform many of the stitches with the quilt sandwich somewhat tight in the hoop.

1. Loosen the screw on the quilt hoop and separate the hoop into its outer and inner rings. Place your layered and hand-basted quilt on the inner ring. Set the outer ring on top. Tighten the screw on the hoop slightly.

2. Turn the hoop over and check for wrinkles on the quilt back. Straighten the wrinkles as required.

3. Tighten the screw until your fabric layers reach the desired tautness.

4. To hold the hoop, use your nonwriting hand. Place your palm against the inside rim or place your thumb over the top of the hoop. Press toward yourself, wedging the hoop against your body. Extend the first or second finger of the same hand to the spot where you wish to begin quilting. Pushing up slightly with this finger will form a small hill on the surface. This hill will aid you as you perform the quilting stitch. (See Stitching Technique, Step 4, on page 35.)

Threading the Needle

Always thread the needle before the thread is cut from the spool. Threading this end seems to reduce the number of knots that form during quilting.

1. Wet the end of the thread in your mouth. Severely flatten the wetted end using your thumbnail and the index finger of your writing hand. Hold the thread between these two fingers so that a mere $1/8$" of thread extends beyond your fingers.

2. Use your other hand to carefully guide the eye of the needle onto the wet thread end. The thickness of the perle cotton will allow you to get only part of the fibers through the eye of the needle. If you have trouble, try threading through the eye from the other side.

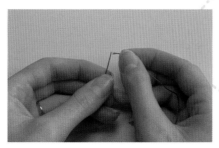

Needle Threading

3. Once you see some of the fibers protruding through the eye of the needle, grasp the fibers with your fingertips and pull the thread through the eye for approximately 10".

4. Cut the thread from the spool about 20" from the needle, for a total thread length of about 30". Needle Magic stitching uses up thread quickly, and you'll appreciate having the extra length.

The Quilter's Knot

The quilter's knot, used for fine hand quilting, also works with perle cotton. To accommodate the extra thread thickness, the thread is wrapped once instead of the usual two or three times. A thimble helps you lodge the knot in the batting.

1. Hold the threaded needle between the thumb and index finger of your writing hand, with the point away from you.

2. Use your other hand to place the end of the thread on the index finger of your writing hand. Press the needle and your thumb against your index finger to hold the thread end in place.

3. Grasp the long part of the thread with your nonwriting hand. Bring the thread up and over the top of the needle in a counter-clockwise direction. Pull the wrapped thread tightly around the needle. Hold the wrapped thread in place with the fleshy part of your thumb on your writing hand.

4. With your nonwriting hand, let go of the thread and grasp the point of the needle. Pull the needle away from yourself while continuing to grasp the wrap with your writing hand. Keep pulling without releasing your grasp to form a perfect small knot near the end of the thread.

5. Wear the thimble on the middle finger of your writing hand. (Some people prefer the first finger or thumb.) Insert the needle into the quilt top and batting about $1/2$" from the point where you wish to start quilting. Bring the needle to the surface at the desired spot. Draw it through and pull up the thread tightly with your nonwriting hand. At the same time, rub your thimble over the knot. The tension will cause the fibers of the fabric to separate and allow the knot to pass through and lodge in the batting layer.

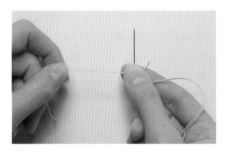

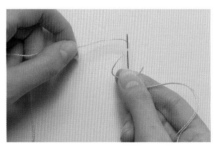

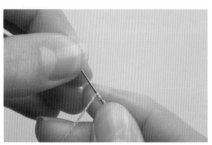

Quilter's Knot Technique

Stitching Technique

To perform Needle Magic stitches, you will be quilting from many different directions. Because the needle enters the fabric at different angles, I find it helpful to push with the side of the thimble, rather than the top. Otherwise the hand position is similar to regular hand quilting. The needle and your writing hand should always be on the surface of the quilt and your non-writing hand should always be under the quilt. Begin by threading the needle and making a quilter's knot. Practice the sequence below in a running stitch before attempting more decorative stitches.

1. Grasp the needle with the thumb and first finger of your writing hand. Place the eye of the needle securely into one of the dimples on the side of the thimble.

Stitching Technique

2. Twist your wrist so that the needle is in a vertical position, pointing straight down into the fabric.

3. Push down with the thimble until the finger of your nonwriting hand on the underside can feel the point of the needle. Let go of the needle with your thumb and first finger of your writing hand. The only things holding the needle should be the thimble and one finger under the quilt.

Using A Thimble

4. Maintain your finger contact with the needle point under the quilt. Do the following three motions simultaneously:

▮ Use the thimble to rock the needle down and parallel to the quilt top.

▮ Push up from below to form a hill. The eye of the needle will now be lower than the top of the hill.

▮ Place the thumb of your writing hand in front of the needle to form a valley.

Rocking The Needle

5. Push with the thimble, nudging the needle forward until the point breaks the surface and you've achieved the desired stitch size.

6. Rock the needle straight up, using the thimble only. Do not push down on the needle as you rock it straight up. The tension on the needle and the fabric will cause the needle point to pierce through the fabric and touch your finger underneath.

7. Repeat Step 4 to complete a second stitch. Repeat Steps 5 and 6 once more. In general, you will be able to carry two or three stitches on the needle at a time. When the needle is full, pull the thread to the top.

8. Repeat Steps 1–7 to continue quilting. When you reach a spot where you can no longer quilt, you can either travel to a position where you can begin quilting again or end the thread.

Traveling

Traveling is the act of moving your needle through the batting layer to a nearby spot where you can begin quilting once again. It's a useful technique for when you have finished quilting a particular section but still have a usable length of thread remaining on the needle. Traveling lets you continue quilting with the same thread, instead of ending off and rethreading the needle.

When the distance between the two areas is less than one needle length, simply pass the needle through the batting to the new position. In fine hand quilting, you'd bring the needle to the surface at the new position and resume quilting. This is fine for short stitches, but I've found it doesn't work for the longer stitches that are typical of Needle Magic. My remedy is to take a short stitch through the back of the quilt before coming up to the top. This ensures that all the stitches—even very long ones—have the same tension and appearance.

Traveling *continued*

In some quilting situations, you will need to travel farther than one needle length allows.

1. Place the point of the needle into the batting layer and travel about half of the needle's length. Bring the point of the needle to the surface.

2. Gently pull the needle through partway and lay it flat on the fabric surface. Leave the eye of the needle concealed.

3. Twist the needle, as if you were resetting a clock hand, so that the eye faces the desired traveling direction. Use your thimble to push on the point of the needle, causing the eye to travel through the batting for about three-quarters of the needle length. Poke the eye of the needle through the fabric surface.

4. Pull the eye end of the needle partway through and lay it flat on the fabric surface. Leave the pointed end of the needle concealed.

5. Twist the needle like a clock hand, so that the point faces the desired direction. Push the eye end with the thimble to bring the needle and thread to the surface in the desired position to continue quilting. Remember to take a small stitch on the back of the quilt first, to establish good thread tension on the quilt front.

Traveling Technique

Ending

Two methods are traditionally used to end the quilting stitch. One method is to bring the thread to the back of the quilt, make a knot next to the surface of the quilt, and pop the knot into the batting layer. The second method is to weave the thread through the batting layer in a figure eight motion around the stitches. (For a similar weaving-in technique, see Wrapping, Steps 1–3, on page 38.)

Straight Stitches

Begin each of these stitches by lodging the knotted end of the thread in the batting.

Traditional Stitch

The traditional stitch is a running stitch similar to the quilting stitch used for fine hand quilting. For my first Needle Magic quilts, I worked stitches approximately $1/4$" long on the surface of the quilt and $1/8$" long on the back of the quilt. As my technique evolved, my surface stitches increased to $3/8$" long. I kept the stitches on the back at $1/8$". The slightly longer length on the quilt front made the stitch pattern and thread color more visible and thus enhanced the embellishment objective.

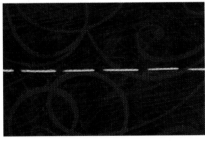

4   3 2   1 4   3 2   1

Traditional Stitch

1. Bring the needle and thread to the surface of the quilt at 1. Proceed along the quilting line approximately $3/8$".

2. Reenter the quilt at 2 and take a $1/8$" stitch on the back of the quilt. Note that although the measured distance of this stitch on the top of the quilt appears to be $1/8$", only $1/16$" of the stitch is usually visible on the back of the quilt.

3. Bring the needle to the surface of the quilt at 3. Proceed along the quilting line approximately $3/8$".

4. Reenter the quilt at 4 and take a $1/8$" stitch on the back of the quilt.

5. Repeat Steps 1–4, stitching from a 1 o'clock to 7 o'clock position if you are right-handed and from an 11 o'clock to 5 o'clock position if you are left-handed, to work the stitch pattern as desired. End off by weaving in.

Short Long Stitch

Use this decorative quilting stitch to navigate tight curves and other areas where clean, smooth lines are required. Two different stitch lengths appear on the front of the work, adding to the visual appeal.

4 3 2   1 4 3 2   1 4 3 2   1

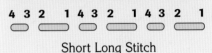

Short Long Stitch

1. Bring the needle and thread to the surface of the quilt at 1. Proceed along the quilting line approximately $3/8$".

2. Reenter the quilt at 2 and take a $1/8$" stitch on the back of the quilt.

3. Bring the needle to the surface of the quilt at 3. Proceed along the quilting line approximately $1/8$".

4. Reenter the quilt at 4 and take a $1/8$" stitch on the back of the quilt.

Short Long Stitch

continued

5. Repeat Steps 1–4, stitching from a 1 o'clock to 7 o'clock position if you are right-handed and from an 11 o'clock to 5 o'clock position if you are left-handed, to work the stitch pattern as desired. It's helpful to develop a repetitive stitching rhythm when working an alternating stitching pattern such as this. For instance, you might carry two stitches on the needle at a time and always pull the needle through at 1. End off by weaving in.

Wrapping

One of the newest and most exciting techniques I have developed is a process I call wrapping. In this technique, a line of traditional stitches is embellished with one or more contrasting threads. Wrapping allows quiltmakers to add many different types and styles of threads, as well as beads and other embellishments, to the quilt surface. As always, experiment with highly contrasting threads for the maximum impact.

At first glance, wrapping appears similar to the embroidery technique of couching, in which one thread is used to anchor another. But it is actually much easier to do. Begin by quilting a line of traditional

or short long stitches. Thread a needle with a contrasting color or style of thread in either a single or a double strand. If you are using a double strand or a thread that is too thick to knot, start at Step 1 and weave in and anchor the ends. If you are using a single strand, make a quilter's knot at the end and skip ahead to Step 4.

1. Enter the batting layer at 1. Weave the needle through the batting, passing through the stitches in a serpentine motion, to complete the first half of a figure eight.

2. Bring the needle to the surface of the quilt at 2. Pull the thread through, but leave the S-shaped tail lodged in the batting, as shown.

3. Tug slightly at the emerging thread to widen the hole in the fabric. Reinsert the pointed end of the needle into the hole. Weave the needle through the batting, passing through the same stitches in the opposite direction, to complete the figure eight.

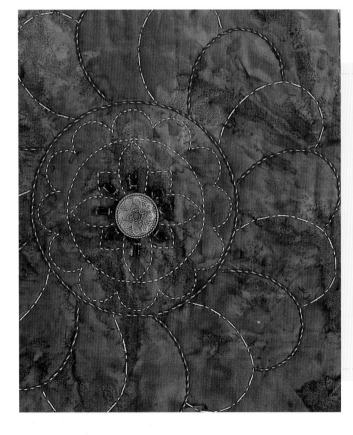

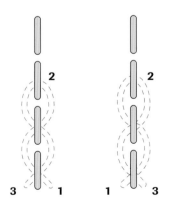

Weaving in the wrapping thread.
Right-Handed   Left-Handed

A double strand of perle cotton wraps twice around each long stitch. The base stitching is light and the **wrapping** thread is dark, for maximum contrast against the medium background fabric. Detail from Linda Potter's *Elegant Embellishments.*

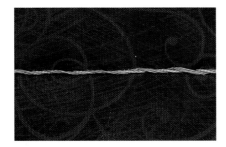

Wrapping

4. Bring the needle to the surface of the quilt at 3. Pass the needle over the stitching line. Slip the needle, eye first, under the first stitch and pull it through. Be careful not to split the thread or enter the fabric.

5. Bring the needle over the top of the line of stitching again. Slip it, eye first, under the desired stitch. Repeat a few more times, then gently pull the thread so that it forms a spiral twist over the stitches.

6. Repeat Step 5 as desired. End off by weaving in.

Experiment with these variations:

▌ Wrap each stitch once.

▌ Wrap each stitch twice.

▌ Wrap with one strand.

▌ Wrap with two strands.

Lacing

Lacing is a traditional embroidery technique. Like wrapping, lacing involves embellishing an existing line of traditional stitches. But instead of crossing over the stitches, a lacing thread weaves back and forth, passing under the stitches, for a flatter appearance.

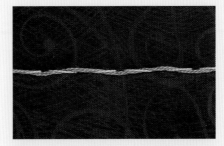

Lacing

1. Weave in the end of the lacing thread (see Wrapping, Steps 1–3, page 38) or use a quilter's knot. Bring the needle to the surface of the quilt, slightly to the left of the stitching line.

2. Pass the needle, eye first, to the right, going under the first stitch in the stitching line. Be careful not to split the thread or enter the fabric.

3. Pass the needle, eye first, to the left, going under the second stitch in the stitching line.

4. Repeat Steps 2 and 3 a few more times, weaving the thread back and forth along the stitching line. Then pull the thread gently to draw up the lacing.

5. Repeat Steps 2–4 as desired. End off by weaving in.

Experiment with these variations:

▌ Lace with a single strand.

▌ Lace with a double strand.

▌ Lace one color thread in one direction and another color thread in the opposite direction.

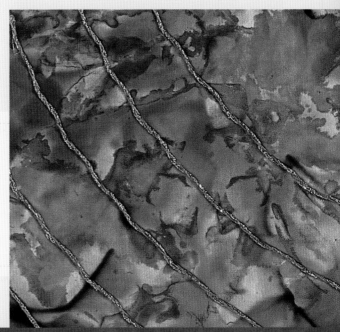

Lacing through the quilting stitches with two strands of heavy metallic thread. Detail from Linda Potter's *Elegant Embellishments*.

Decorative Stitches

Begin each of these stitches by lodging the knotted end of the thread in the batting.

Herringbone Stitch

The herringbone stitch is a traditional embroidery stitch. Long stitches on the face of the work and short stitches on the back make the herringbone stitching path perfect for Needle Magic. It looks especially decorative along the edge of a seam or an appliqué, and it can even be used to tack down the quilt binding.

Note that for right-handed stitchers, the needle moves from right to left, but the herringbone pattern itself advances from left to right. For left-handed stitchers, the needle moves from left to right and the herringbone pattern advances from right to left.

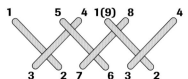

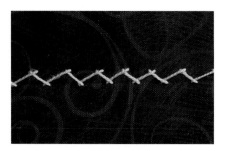

Herringbone Stitch, Right-Handed

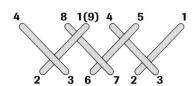

Herringbone Stitch, Left-Handed

1. Bring the needle and thread to the surface of the quilt at 1.

2. Reenter the quilt at 2, take a short stitch on the back of the quilt, and pull the needle and thread to the surface at 3.

3. Reenter the quilt at 4, take a short stitch on the back of the quilt, and bring the needle and thread to the surface at 5.

4. Reenter the quilt at 6, take a short stitch on the back of the quilt, and bring the needle and thread to the surface at 7.

5. Reenter the quilt at 8, take a short stitch on the back of the quilt, and bring the needle and thread to the surface at 1 (or 9).

6. Repeat the pattern established in Steps 2–5 as desired. End off.

Experiment with these variations:

■ Increase the stitch length on the underside of the quilt (between 2 and 3, 4 and 5, 6 and 7, and so forth).

■ Increase the stitch length on the top of the quilt (between 1 and 2, 3 and 4, 5 and 6, and so forth).

■ Use varying stitch lengths on the underside only.

■ Use varying stitch lengths on the top surface only.

■ Use varying stitch lengths on both the underside and the top surface.

Herringbone Stitch Variations

I especially love the appearance of herringbone stitch along the binding. Here, the stitch performs a triple function. It tacks down the binding, holds the quilt layers in place, and embellishes the edge of the quilt. For this technique, quilt the surface of the quilt and trim the batting and backing even with the quilt top. Sew the binding to the back of the quilt (instead of the front). Fold the binding onto the front of the quilt and tack in place using the herringbone stitch.

Herringbone stitch along the binding of Linda Potter's *Pumpkin Party.*

Blanket Stitch

The blanket stitch is another embroidery stitch that is especially decorative along the edge of a seamline or an appliqué. In blanket stitch, you move the needle toward yourself. The stitch itself advances from left to right for right-handed stitchers and from right to left for left-handed stitchers. The stitches should be of a uniform size and spacing.

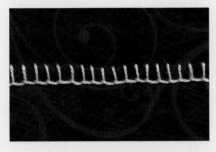

Blanket Stitch, Right-Handed

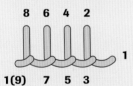

Blanket Stitch, Left-Handed

1. Bring the needle and thread to the surface of the quilt at 1.

2. Reenter the quilt at 2, take a stitch on the back of the quilt, and pierce the needle to the surface at 3. Make sure the thread emerging from point 1 is under the tip of the needle. Pull the needle through and over the thread to complete the stitch. Maintain a consistent tension; do not pull too tightly, or the stitch will roll up.

3. Reenter the quilt at 4, take a stitch on the back of the quilt, and pierce the needle to the surface at 5. Make sure the thread is under the tip of the needle and pull the needle through, as before, to complete the stitch.

4. Reenter the quilt at 6, take a stitch on the back of the quilt, and pierce the needle to the surface at 7. Make sure the thread is under the tip of the needle and pull the needle through, as before, to complete the stitch.

5. Repeat the sequence established in Steps 2–4 as desired. Take a small stitch to the underside to tack down the final stitch (similar to an embroidery couching stitch). End off.

Myrtle Stitch

The Myrtle is a blanket stitch variation dedicated to my grandmother Myrtle Deamud (1896–1997). Grandma used this stitch extensively for *Broderie Perse* appliqué from the 1930s to 1975, when she completed her last quilt for the birth of our son. Because the stitches in the Myrtle are various lengths, it is actually a bit easier to stitch than the blanket stitch, where the stitches are of a uniform size. The stitching advances from left to right for right-handed stitchers and from right to left for left-handed stitchers, just as in the blanket stitch.

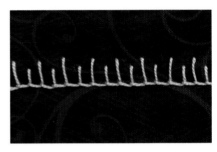

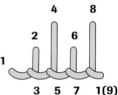

Myrtle Stitch, Right-Handed

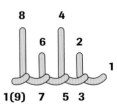

Myrtle Stitch, Left-Handed

1. Bring the needle to the surface of the quilt at 1.

Myrtle Stitch *continued*

2. Reenter the quilt at 2, take a stitch on the back of the quilt, and pierce the needle to the surface at 3. Make sure the thread emerging from point 1 is under the tip of the needle. Pull the needle through and over the thread to complete the stitch. Maintain a consistent tension; do not pull too tightly, or the stitch will roll up.

3. Reenter the quilt at 4, take a stitch on the back of the quilt, and pierce the needle to the surface at 5. Make sure the thread is under the tip of the needle and pull the needle through, as before, to complete the stitch.

4. Reenter the quilt at 6, take a stitch on the back of the quilt, and pierce the needle to the surface at 7. Make sure the thread is under the tip of the needle and pull the needle through, as before, to complete the stitch. The stitch length between 6 and 7 should be the same as the stitch length between 2 and 3.

5. Reenter the quilt at 8, take a stitch on the back of the quilt, and pierce the needle to the surface at 1 (9). Make sure the thread is under the tip of the needle and pull the needle through, as before, to complete the stitch. The stitch length between 8 and 9 should be the same as the stitch length between 4 and 5.

6. Repeat Steps 4 and 5 as desired, alternating between the two stitch lengths. Take a small stitch to the underside to tack down the final stitch (similar to an embroidery couching stitch). End off.

The Myrtle allows for lots of creative possibilities. The length of the stitches can be varied at any point and on an incremental scale. By combining three or more stitch lengths in your stitching sequence, you can achieve artistic results that go far beyond the scope of the blanket stitch on which the Myrtle is based.

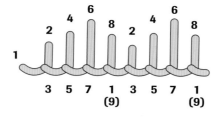

Magic Fern Stitch

The Magic Fern is based on the fern stitch used in traditional embroidery. This stitch is especially decorative along the edge of a seamline or as a free-flowing meandering design. I've modified the embroidery stitching sequence to accommodate the quilting function. I find that as I teach this stitch my students interpret my sense of direction in various ways. Most right-handed stitchers work the stitch from a 5 o'clock to 11 o'clock position, and most left-handed stitchers work the stitch from a 7 o'clock to 1 o'clock position. Work in whatever direction is best for you.

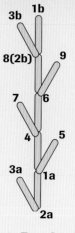

Magic Fern Stitch

1. Bring the needle and thread to the surface of the quilt at 1a.

2. Reenter the quilt at 2a, take a stitch on the back of the quilt, and bring the needle and thread to the surface of the quilt at 3a.

3. Reenter the quilt at 2a, pass through the batting layer only, and bring the needle and thread to the surface of the quilt at 4.

4. Reenter the quilt at 1a, take a stitch on the back of the quilt, and bring the needle and thread to the surface of the quilt at 5.

5. Reenter the quilt at 1a, pass through the batting layer only, and bring the needle and thread to the surface of the quilt at 6.

6. Reenter the quilt at 4, take a stitch on the back of the quilt, and bring the needle and thread to the surface of the quilt at 7.

7. Reenter the quilt at 4, pass through the batting layer only, and bring the needle and thread to the surface of the quilt at 8 (2b).

8. Reenter the quilt at 6, take a stitch on the back of the quilt, and bring the needle and thread to the surface of the quilt at 9.

9. Reenter the quilt at 6, pass through the batting layer only, and bring the needle and thread to the surface of the quilt at 1b.

10. Reenter the quilt at 8 (2b), take a stitch on the back of the quilt, and bring the needle and thread to the surface of the quilt at 3b.

11. Repeat Steps 3–10 as desired. End off.

The Magic Fern stitch used for quilting. Detail from Linda Potter's *Evening Lilies.*

Troubleshooting

There's not too much that can go wrong with these playful stitches. Here are a few pointers to keep in mind.

■ Strive for needle control, but don't obsess. Remember, with this technique, quirky stitches add to the character and charm of the piece.

■ Stop stitching while you still have enough thread in the needle to end off properly.

■ Take advantage of a varying stitch length as you approach seam junctures. When you are quilting in-the-ditch and have about 1" to go, gauge the stitch length so that you can enter at the exact point where the seams meet. This way, you can avoid stitching through bulky layers of fabric.

Appliqué

As a quilter who also loves doing appliqué, I was torn between the two. Traditional needleturn appliqué is time-consuming, and it seemed that whenever I embarked on an appliqué project, I ended up thinking, "It's taking too long. I could be quilting." It occurred to me that if I fused my appliqué shapes in place first, I might be able to appliqué and quilt in one step.

To try out my idea, I cut and pressed strips of fusible material around the edges of an appliqué. My intention was to avoid bulk underneath the appliqué, but the strips were too unwieldy. Next, I made an outline of the shape and cut a hole in the middle. This one-piece fusible "doughnut" gave me appliqués that were neatly fused on the edge and soft in the center. Here was a shape I could appliqué, quilt, and embellish all at the same time.

Supplies

In addition to the supplies for embellishment quilting (see pages 14–18), you will need:

■ A quilt pattern—Look for a small quilt size and large, simple appliqué shapes. Decorative wall quilts are ideal. Avoid bed-sized quilts (you'll be stitching forever) or any item that would suffer wear and tear from ordinary handling. Stay away from tiny, intricate appliqués. Patterns with a mix of large and small appliqués can be used if you substitute stitching or beadwork for the smaller details.

■ Tracing paper—Use artist-quality tracing paper, sold at art supply and craft stores.

■ A heavy-duty fusible web—Choose a product designed for fusing without machine stitching. The appliqué shapes are placed under a great deal of stress prior to quilting, and the fusible web must be extremely durable.

■ Teflon pressing sheets or pressing papers—Be sure you have two sheets. You will sandwich your fusible web and fabric shapes between the protective sheets so that the pieces don't accidentally fuse to your iron or ironing board.

■ Small utility scissors—Choose a pair with small, pointed tips and extra-sharp blades to cut the fusible web and fabric appliqués.

Appliqué Exercises

I designed my quilted table runner *Random Hearts* to be a sampler of appliqué and embellishment techniques. The following exercises, based on the *Random Hearts* quilt pattern, illustrate how to prepare the appliqués for three overlapping hearts. (For complete project instructions, see page 63.)

As in any appliqué technique, the process of preparing the appliqués can seem tedious. If you persevere, you'll experience the joy of being able to appliqué, quilt, and embellish simultaneously. I encourage you to work through these exercises. They will prepare you for different appliqué situations that you are likely to encounter and will give you a head start on the *Random Hearts* quilt project as well.

Appliqué detail from Linda Potter's *Serenity*.

Exercise 1:
The Placement Guide

A placement guide is used to help position the appliqués on the fabric background. Quiltmakers who do traditional appliqué often use clear upholstery vinyl for their placement guides. Because the Needle Magic technique requires pressing a hot iron on top of the placement guide, I use artist's tracing paper instead.

The Placement Guide

1. Trace the pattern.
Lay tracing paper on the overlapping hearts pattern (page 68). Trace the pattern lines with a pencil or pen. Label this side of the tracing as Placement Guide.

Tracing the Pattern

2. Identify the appliqué order.
Determine how the appliqués will overlap one another. Number the shapes (1, 2, 3, and so forth) in the order that they will be appliquéd. The highest number is the shape that appears on top (the piece that will be appliquéd last).

3. Reverse the pattern.
Turn the tracing over, so that the mirror image of the pattern faces up. Use this mirror image pattern to make all appliqué tracings and templates. The pattern will revert back to its right-side-up position during the fusible web process.

The Mirror Image Pattern

Exercise 2:
Making a Template

Sometimes the same appliqué shape appears multiple times in a quilt pattern. In the *Random Hearts* Quilt Diagram (page 65), Heart *b* appears several times. It makes sense to make a plastic template for shapes that repeat like this. A plastic template can be used many times over. It helps streamline the appliqué process.

1. Mark the template plastic.
Lay a piece of heavy-duty template plastic on the mirror image pattern. Trace the pattern outline with a pencil.

2. Cut out the template.
Use small utility scissors. To ensure accurate cutting, hold the template plastic in your nonwriting hand and cut on the *inside edge* of the marked line. Keep your writing hand stationary. Use your nonwriting hand to slowly turn the template plastic and feed it into the path of the scissors.

Right-handed cutting position. Cut in a clockwise direction, with the marked line to the left of the scissors blade. If you are left-handed, cut in a counterclockwise direction, with the marked line to the right of the scissors blade.

Exercise 3:
Making an Appliqué

Follow these instructions for single appliqué shapes that are not repeated frequently or for shapes that form the top layer of an overlapping design. You'll be making the appliqué for Heart **b**.

1. Mark the fusible web.

Mark the appliqué shape on the paper side of the fusible web. If you are marking more than one shape, allow at least $1/2$" of space between the pieces.

Pattern method. Lay the fusible web, paper side up, on top of the mirror image pattern. Trace the outline of the appliqué shape with a mechanical pencil.

Template method. Lay the template on the paper side of the fusible web. Trace around the edges of the template with a mechanical pencil.

2. Cut out the fusible web doughnut.

First, cut about $1/4$" *outside* the marked outline, to isolate the appliqué. Then cut $1/8$" *inside* the marked outline. The $1/8$" inside measurement is fairly critical to the appliqué process. If you cut $1/16$" inside the drawn line, you run the risk of not having enough fusible web for the appliqués to adhere properly. If you cut $1/4$" inside the drawn line, you may have difficulty stitching through the extra layer. While you don't have to cut precisely $1/8$" from the line, do familiarize yourself with the $1/8$" measurement and attempt to cut each piece as close to it as you can.

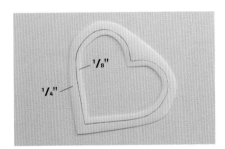

The Fusible Web Doughnut

3. Fuse the doughnut to the fabric.
Layer the following four pieces on an ironing board:

■ Pressing sheet or pressing paper

■ Fabric, wrong side up

■ Fusible web doughnut, paper side up

■ Pressing sheet or pressing paper

I find that placing the doughnut shape on the bias of the fabric makes the cut edge less prone to raveling. Follow the manufacturer's instructions for iron temperature and pressing time to adhere the fusible web to the fabric. If you don't follow the manufacturer's pressing instructions, the pieces may not fuse properly.

4. Cut out the appliqué.
Cut on the marked line. You will be trimming off the entire $1/4$" fusible web allowance outside the trim and leaving $1/8$" of fusible web inside the line.

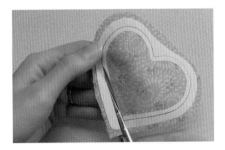

Cutting the Appliqué

If you traced around a template, remember that the marked outline is slightly larger than your original pattern. Be sure to cut on the inside edge of the line to retain the original size.

Exercise 4:
Overlapping Appliqués

When an appliqué has another shape overlapping it, you can compensate by adding what I call an extension. The extension provides a bit of extra fabric to go underneath the appliqué on top. By cutting off the $^1/_8$" margin of fusible web on the extension, you can keep the overlapping layers as soft and pliable as possible. The tracing and cutting processes are slightly different from the appliqué instructions above. You'll be making the appliqués for Hearts *d* and *e* (Hearts 1 and 2 on the placement guide, page 46).

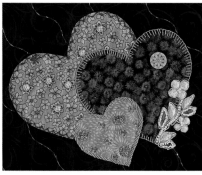

Overlapping heart appliqués with multiple stitches, beads, and trims.

1. Mark the fusible web.
Lay the fusible web, paper side up, on the mirror image of the placement guide. Trace around one shape with a solid line; use a dashed line to indicate an edge overlapped by another shape. Draw a solid line at least $^1/_2$" beyond the dashed line for the extension.

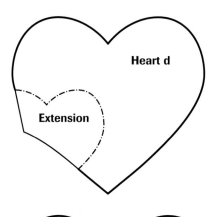

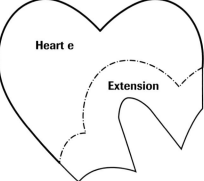

Shapes with Extensions

2. Cut out the fusible web doughnut.
Cut about $^1/_4$" *outside* the marked solid outline to isolate the appliqué. Then cut $^1/_8$" *inside* the marked solid outline. Ignore the dashed line when cutting. Note that the $^1/_4$" outside margin doesn't have to follow the contours exactly.

The Fusible Web Doughnut with Extension

3. Fuse the doughnut to the wrong side of the fabric.
See Making an Appliqué, Step 3 (page 47).

4. Cut out the appliqué.
See Making an Appliqué, Step 4 (page 47). Then trim off the $^1/_8$" of fusible web at the end of the extension. Repeat Steps 1–4 for each shape in the design.

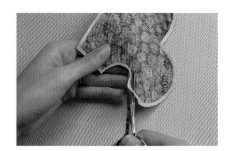

Trimming the Extension

Preparing the Quilt Top

In traditional hand appliqué, the handwork is done first and then the appliquéd blocks are pieced together into the quilt top. Needle Magic appliqué requires a different approach. The piecing and borders come first, to complete the quilt top, and then the appliqués are added. In this sequence, you layer and baste the quilt top immediately after fusing the appliqués.

Perle cotton stitches along both sides of a narrow fused stem can appear heavy and clumsy. For a more delicate look, use traditional bias-cut strips for stems and appliqué them by hand. Sew the stems to the blocks or quilt top before fusing the other appliqués. If a leaf is to appear under the stem, pin the leaf in place, appliqué the stem over it, and complete the fusing later.

Fusing

Once you have prepared an appliqué placement guide and shapes (see Appliqué Exercises on pages 46–48), fusing the shapes to the quilt top is a simple process. Arrange the quilt top on an ironing board, right side up, so that the background fabric for your appliqués lies flat. If the area to be appliquéd is large, you may have to work in sections.

Pull the paper backing from each shape. Place the shapes, right side up, in their approximate positions on the background. Lay the placement guide (remember, this is the right-side-up tracing) over the pieces to check their position. Use a few straight pins to secure the placement guide to the quilt background and ironing board cover. Once the placement guide is secure, slide your hand under it and move the shapes around until they match the drawing on the tracing. Make sure no extensions are peeking out from behind the appliqués. Some last minute trimming might be required.

Adjusting the Position

Follow the manufacturer's instructions for iron temperature and pressing time to fuse the appliqués in place. Use the tracing paper as a pressing sheet, removing the pins one at a time as you press.

Basting

After all the appliqué shapes are fused to the quilt top, take a few moments to evaluate the overall design, including your intended stitching design. As in traditional appliqué, there may be spots where several layers of fabric overlap. Stitching through these multiple layers can be difficult. To ensure easier stitching later on, you may want to cut away portions of the background and appliqué shapes.

Proceed with caution as you tackle this delicate surgery. Trimming out bulky areas from the background can weaken the surrounding fibers. The appliqué shapes may loosen. Reinforce the potential trouble spots by hand basting around the edges of the appliqués. Since your ultimate objective is embellishment, and since embellished quilts are used primarily as wallhangings or for decoration, a weaker background does not present a long-term problem, just a temporary challenge.

Now you can layer the quilt top, batting, and backing and baste the layers together. Use long hand-basting stitches and tack down stray appliqué shapes or loose edges as you go. Regardless of the care you take with this technique, there are times when the fusible web insists on pulling away from the background. Extra basting stitches will hold the shapes in place until you have an opportunity to complete the embellishment quilting.

Appliqué Stitches

After experimenting with various embroidery stitches, I have found four that I prefer to use for embellishment appliqué: herringbone stitch, blanket stitch, the Myrtle stitch, and a stitch of my own devising called the "angled overcast stitch."

The herringbone, blanket, and Myrtle stitches are worked pretty much as they are for Needle Magic. The only requirement is that the needle enter the appliqué shape from the surface of the quilt. This allows you to pierce through the appliqué shape toward the back of the quilt. If the needle passes from the bottom up through the appliqué, you run the risk of pulling the shape loose from the background. The part of each stitch that enters the background fabric only should be as close as possible to the edge of the appliqué.

Begin each of these stitches by lodging the knotted end of the thread in the batting.

Herringbone Stitch

Refer to the basic herringbone stitch instructions on page 40. For the appliqué technique, hold the work so that the appliqué shape is below the stitching line. Stitch from left to right if you are right-handed and from right to left if you are left-handed.

Keeping the stitching neat and even around curves, corners, and points can be tricky. As you go around an inside curve or corner, such as the inverted V at the top of a heart, space the stitches on the background closer together and the stitches on the appliqué farther apart. As you go around an outside curve or corner, space the stitches on the appliqué closer together and the stitches on the background farther apart.

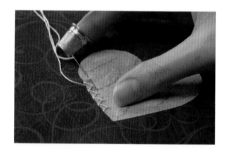

Herringbone Stitch Appliqué

Blanket Stitch and Myrtle Stitch

Refer to the basic blanket stitch and Myrtle stitch instructions on pages 41 and 42. To appliqué, hold the work so that the appliqué shape is above the stitching line. Stitch from left to right if you are right-handed and from right to left if you are left-handed.

Follow the same spacing principles as for the herringbone stitch: On inside curves and corners, go close together on the background and farther apart on the appliqué. On outside curves and corners, do the reverse.

Blanket Stitch Appliqué

Angled Overcast Stitch

While the execution of this stitch is extremely simple, the final effect can be especially dynamic. Hold the work with the appliqué on the right if you are right-handed; on the left if you are left-handed.

1. Bring the needle and the thread to the surface of the quilt at 1.

2. Enter the appliqué shape at 2 and take a stitch on the back of the quilt.

3. Bring the needle to the surface of the quilt at 3 so that the needle runs perpendicular to the edge of the appliqué, as if to form a cross. Pull the needle and thread through to make an angled stitch between 1 and 2.

4. Enter the appliqué shape at 4, and take a stitch on the back of the quilt.

5. Bring the needle to the surface of the quilt at 5, check for the "cross," and pull the needle and thread through to make an angled stitch between 3 and 4.

6. Repeat Steps 4 and 5 to work the stitching pattern. End off.

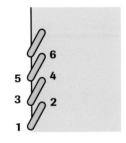

Angled Overcast Stitch
Right-Handed

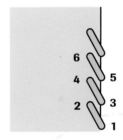

Angled Overcast Stitch
Left-Handed

Angled Overcast Stitch *continued*

Angled Overcast Stitch Appliqué

The size and direction of the angled overcast stitch can be varied. Just change the angle of the needle between the 2 and 3 position and the 4 and 5 position. With this variation, the angle of the stitch becomes more acute.

Acute-Angled Overcast Stitch

Herringbone stitch, blanket stitch variation, and acute-angled overcast stitch. Detail from Linda Potter's *Random Hearts*.

Beading

I n the early 1990s, while a member of the Austin Area Quilt Guild (an organization I fondly refer to as one of the best quilting graduate schools in the country), I became enamored with beads. Many of my fellow guild members took classes in jewelry making on the side. It was through them that I began to visualize the use of beads on my quilts.

For several years I collected beads, but time constraints prevented me from putting them to use. When I completed the quilt top for Mrs. Goose Dresses for Spring, it seemed to call out for beaded embellishment. Since I knew nothing about beading and hadn't seen any quilts with beads on them, I invented my own beading techniques.

You've probably heard the designer's maxim "Less is more." I pare things down even further by adding "and more is too much." I apply a minimalist philosophy to both my quilt designs and my use of beads. I prefer to select and place a few special beads, allowing them to make a quiet contribution rather than to become a screaming focal point. Even though I accumulate beads at the speed of lightning, I use them sparingly.

Supplies

In addition to quilting and appliqué supplies (pages 14–18 and 45), you will need:

- Beads
- Bead tray
- Silamide beading thread
- Size 10 sharps

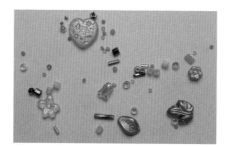

Assorted Beads

Collecting beads for a quilt is a bit like collecting fabric and quilting stencils: the more variety, the better. Beads come in all shapes and sizes. They can be plastic, metal, glass, semiprecious stones, and even crystals. Some beads are shiny, some are flat, some are transparent, and some are opaque. I'm attracted to unusual colors and luminous effects. As you begin your collection, study the shape of the bead and the location of the hole in the bead. Consider how the bead will lie on the surface of a quilt and whether you will like the effect.

For quilting embellishment, I prefer beads 8mm and larger. These beads have a hole large enough to take a threaded embroidery/crewel needle. This way, I can add beads as I stitch. Occasionally I use bugle beads. Some bugle beads have smooth finished edges, but others are cut from a long tube of glass and have sharp edges that may ultimately cut your thread. Threading a smooth bead at each end of a rough bugle bead helps handle this problem.

When the hole in a bead is too small to accommodate an embroidery needle and perle cotton, I use a size 10 sharp and a tightly twisted beading thread called Silamide. When doubled, Silamide provides a strong base for beading with smaller beads. It is also good for securing randomly placed single beads. I don't recommend using beading needles for quilted embellishment work. Fine, long, and thin beading needles bend easily when worked through fabric and batting.

Bead trays will help you keep your beads sorted as you work. I use a white ceramic dish. The white background helps me see the beads clearly. The dish is shallow, so it's easy to reach in and slip a bead onto the needle and then proceed to the next stitch or bead.

Is It Colorfast?

Some beads, believe it or not, are not colorfast. Beads lined with color are especially susceptible to fading. To test for colorfastness, place a few beads in a white Styrofoam cup with a small amount of very hot water and some detergent. Leave the beads for approximately one hour. Then remove the beads, let them dry, and compare their color to those still in the container.

A bead necklace makes an understated fashion statement. More beads adorn the floral print dress and background fabric. Detail from *Mrs. Goose Dresses for Spring* by Linda Potter. Original pattern from *The Warmth of Wool and the Fun of Flannel* by Karen Roossien (Four Corners Designs, 1997).

Auditioning

Selecting beads for a quilt is similar to selecting fabric and thread. You have to try out different bead and thread color combinations.

Start by thinking about how you would like to use the beads. Will you work them in as you quilt, using perle cotton, or will they be applied afterward with Silamide thread? To audition beads, slip a few on a strand of thread and lay the thread over the surface to be quilted. You can also place a few beads directly on the surface. Observe how the beads interact with the fabrics and fibers.

Even after beads have passed an audition, applying them to the quilt is still often a matter of trial and error. For me, beading is "play time." I find myself stitching on various beads and then happily removing them to try yet another composition until I find my favorite sequence.

For hassle-free beading, try this sequence:

1. Quilting without beads
2. Quilting with beads
3. Binding
4. Other beading

Beading As You Quilt

According to the few books I have found on the subject, most quilters who use beads prefer to bead their quilts first and then perform the quilting process. I'm just the opposite. To me, quilting on a beaded surface is a complicated process. Threads so easily become tangled in the beads. My solution is to quilt and bead simultaneously. What could be simpler than slipping a bead or two onto the needle as you work the perle cotton embellishment? Beads added in this way can decorate the short long, herringbone, blanket, the Magic Fern, and wrapped stitches.

Short Long Stitch with Beads. The butterfly beads and accent beads on top of the quilting stitches are added later. Detail from Linda Potter's *Elegant Embellishments*.

The Magic Fern Stitch with Beads. Beads intensify the decorative impact of the Magic Fern stitch in this highly stylized heart. Detail from Linda Potter's *Random Hearts*.

Wrapped stitches encrusted with dozens of beads create a radiant sunset. A few fish-shaped beads swim through the water. Detail from *My Dream Vacation* by Judy Oberkrom and Linda Potter.

Beading After Quilting

Beading after quilting lets me see how a bead interacts with the other surface decoration. I can attach beads exactly where I want them, taking advantage of the quilt sandwich so that knots and traveled stitches lodge in the batting layer. Small stitches and threads do occasionally find their way to the back of the quilt, but since my primary goal is to create an interesting visual surface on the quilt front, I do not obsess over them. Patterned fabrics on the quilt back do a wonderful camouflage job, should someone look.

For beading after quilting, use Silamide thread and a size 10 sharp. Thread the needle, cut the thread from the spool approximately 36" long, and bring the ends together in a quilter's knot. This gives you an extra-strong double thread to work with. Some beading experts advise reentering the beads as you sew, for extra security. In my opinion, quilts with beaded embellishment are meant for display, not heavy handling, and a doubled thread provides the necessary durability.

Beading a Line

Traditional beading dictates that a line of beads should lie flat on the surface and be secured every third to fifth bead. I don't always follow the rules. Sometimes I allow the beaded strand to be raised or even looped.

1. Bring the needle and thread to the surface of the quilt.

2. Load one or more beads onto the needle.

3. Reenter the quilt and secure with a tiny stitch on the back of the quilt.

4. Travel to the next location and bring the needle to the surface.

5. Repeat Steps 1–4 as desired. End off.

Single Beads

Use your bead "play time" to finesse your arrangement. When you are satisfied, pin each bead in place until you can sew it securely. The process of adding a solitary bead is somewhat like sewing on a button. I secure the bead with two to three passes through the hole. If the beads are close together, you can travel through the batting from one location to the next.

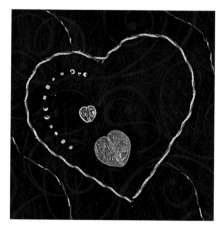

Single beads appear to float within a wrapped heart outline. Detail from Linda Potter's *Random Hearts*.

Accentuate a printed image. Beads sewn to the surface highlight the bird in a printed fabric. Detail from Linda Potter's *Random Hearts*.

The Stop Stitch

Randomly placed beads can also be secured with a technique called the stop stitch. You'll need two beads—a decorative bead and a smaller bead.

1. Bring the needle and thread to the surface of the quilt.

2. Load the larger bead and then the smaller bead onto the needle. Pull the needle through.

3. Insert the needle back through the larger bead, going in the opposite direction.

4. Reenter the quilt at or near the starting point and secure with a tiny stitch on the back of the quilt, then travel to the next location or end off.

5. Repeat Steps 1–4 as desired.

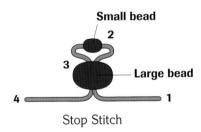

Stop Stitch

Special Effects

The creative use of beads knows no bounds. There are many interesting effects you can achieve. Artists like to combine different shapes, sizes, and colors together in a mixture called "bead soup." I like to apply bead soup in a random way, as if someone has sprinkled the beads across the surface. I call this technique "bead sprinkles." I also use beads to accentuate shapes, add sparkle, and create details that would be hard or time-consuming to add in other ways.

Add bead sprinkles. Mix up a bead soup to go with your quilt and sprinkle it across the surface. These sparkly flowers are from Leanne Baraban's *Garden Oasis*.

Add "missing" details. Beadwork and a ruched flower replace some of the appliqué details in this Robyn Pandolph design. Detail from Linda Potter's *Serenity*.

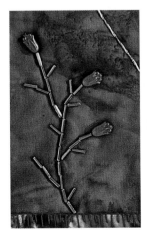

Make pictures. Use different bead colors, sizes, and shapes to paint a bead picture. *Left:* Tulip-shaped beads and bugle beads become flowers with stems. Detail from Linda Potter's *Elegant Embellishments*. *Right:* A beaded butterfly from Linda Potter's *Night Flight*.

Fall Shadows

by Linda Potter ❖ 1997, 69" x 57"

Here's yet another example of my "less is more" philosophy. As quiltmakers, we often feel obligated to overquilt. **Fall Shadows** uses minimal quilting to make strong and dramatic visual impact. A few artfully placed quilting lines and a group of leaf blocks tossed in various directions are all it takes to create the illusion of movement. You can almost hear the leaves rustling in the wind.

Cotton fabrics, #8 perle cotton, Thermore batting. Machine-pieced, hand-quilted.

Materials

Leaves: $^1/_8$ yard each of
  14 different fabrics
Background and outer border:
  4 yards
Inner border and binding: 1 yard
Backing: $4^1/_8$ yards
Batting: 71" x 57"
Solid color rayon thread
  (darker than leaf fabrics, for
  satin stitch stems)

You'll also need freezer paper,
heavy-duty template plastic, a
fabric marker, and a Flexicurve
design tool.

Cutting

Leaf Blocks (12)

❏ From each leaf fabric, cut 1
crosswise strip 2" wide. Subcut
each strip into:
  2 rectangles 2" x 10". Label as *a*.
  10 squares 2" x 2". Label as *b*.
❏ From the background fabric,
cut 10 crosswise strips $2^3/_4$" wide.
Subcut into:
  24 rectangles $2^3/_4$" x $3^1/_2$".
    Label as *c*.
  48 rectangles $2^3/_4$" x 2".
    Label as *d*.
  24 rectangles $2^3/_4$" x $4^1/_4$".
    Label as *e*.
  12 squares $2^3/_4$" x $2^3/_4$".
    Label as *f*.
❏ From the background fabric,
cut 2 crosswise strips $4^1/_4$" wide.
Subcut into:
  12 squares $4^1/_4$" x $4^1/_4$".
    Label as *g*.

Background Blocks (27)

❏ Cut 8 crosswise strips $3^1/_2$"
wide. Subcut into:
  12 rectangles $3^1/_2$" x $9^1/_2$".
    Label as *A*.
  8 rectangles $3^1/_2$" x $12^1/_2$".
    Label as *B*.
  3 rectangles $3^1/_2$" x $15^1/_2$".
    Label as *D*.
❏ Cut 2 crosswise strips $6^1/_2$"
wide. Subcut into:
  3 rectangles $6^1/_2$" x $12^1/_2$".
    Label as *C*.
  1 rectangle $6^1/_2$" x $9^1/_2$".
    Label as *E*.

Inner Border and Binding

❏ Cut 5 crosswise strips $1^1/_2$"
wide. Sew the strips together end
to end with bias seams. Subcut
into:
  2 strips $1^1/_2$" x $51^1/_2$" for the top
    and bottom inner borders.
  2 strips $1^1/_2$" x $39^1/_2$" for the side
    inner borders.
❏ Cut 7 crosswise strips $2^1/_4$"
wide for the binding.

Outer Borders

❏ Cut 2 lengthwise strips $8^1/_2$" x
$55^1/_2$" for the side outer borders.
❏ Cut 2 lengthwise strips $8^1/_2$" x
$53^1/_2$" for the top and bottom outer
borders.

Stem Preparation

1. Trace the stem pattern (page
62) onto template plastic. Cut out
the template. (See Exercise 2 on
page 46.)

2. Cut a 6" x 6" square of freezer
paper. Place fabric *g* right side down
on the ironing board. Place the
freezer paper on the fabric, waxy
side down. Press with a hot, dry
iron for a few seconds, or until the
freezer paper adheres to the wrong
side of the fabric. Lift the fused
pieces from the ironing board.

3. Lay the fused pieces, fabric side
up. Place the stem template on the
fabric, aligning at three corners.
Use a fabric marker to trace a
curved line from **x** to **y**. Repeat
Steps 2 and 3 to mark 12 *g* pieces
total. Reverse the template (flip it
over) for some, to vary the image.
(I used the template right side up
for 5 blocks and reversed for 7
blocks.)

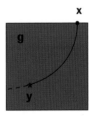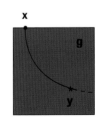

4. Thread the top of the sewing machine with rayon thread. Adjust the tension to pull the top thread toward the underside of the fabric. Set the stitch length at a position slightly longer than the satin stitch setting. Set the stitch width at the smallest zigzag setting. Stitch from **x** to **y**, gradually increasing the zigzag setting so that it reaches its maximum width at **Y**. Pull the threads to the underside and tie them off. Gently remove the freezer paper.

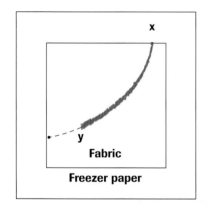

Leaf Stem Block

Leaf Block Assembly

1. Sew the *a* strips together in random pairs. Press as desired. Make 12 assorted strip sets. Subcut into 2" segments until you have 36 *aa* segments.

2. Select 1 *b* and 1 *d*. Use the Connector method (page 93) to piece *b* to one end of *d,* as shown. Make 24 *bd* units. Repeat, reversing the *b* piece, to make 24 *bdr* units.

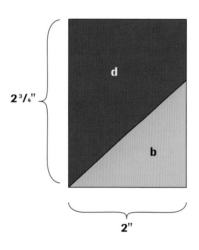

2³/₄"

2"

Unit *bd*
Make 24.

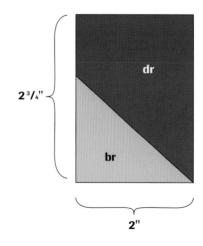

2³/₄"

2"

Unit *bdr*
Make 24.

3. Select 2 *b* and 1 *c*. Use the Connector method to stitch 1 *b* to *c*, as shown. Press. Repeat to join the other *b* to *c*. Make 24 *bbc* units.

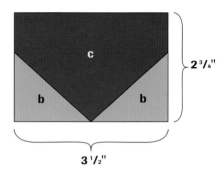

2³/₄"

3¹/₂"

Unit *bbc*
Make 24.

4. For Unit I, lay out 1 *aa*, 1 *bbc*, and 1 *e*. Sew *aa* to *bbc*. Press toward *bbc*. Add *e*. Press toward *e*. Make 12 units.

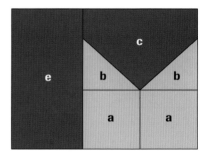

Unit I
Make 12.

5. For Unit II, lay out 1 *aa*, 1 *b*, 1 *bd*, 1 *bdr*, and 1 *g,* as shown. Note the orientation of the stem in piece *g*; 5 stems will be right side up, 7 will be reversed. Sew *aa* to *bd*. Press toward *aa*. Sew *b* to *bdr*. Press toward *b*. Join *b*bdr* to *g*. Press toward *g*. Join the two sections together. Press toward *aa*bd*. Make 12 units.

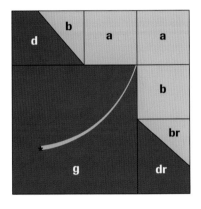

Unit II
Make 12.

6. For Unit III, lay out 1 *aa*, 1 *b*, 1 *bbc*, 1 *bd*, 1 *bdr*, 1 *e*, and 1 *f*. Sew *bdr* to *f*. Press toward *f*. Sew *b* to *bd*. Press toward *b*. Sew *aa* to *bbc*. Press toward *c*. Join the three sections and *e* together. Press toward *e*. Make 12 units.

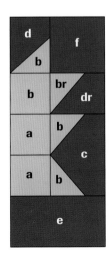

Unit III
Make 12.

7. Lay out units I, II, and III, as shown. Sew Unit I to Unit II. Press toward Unit I. Join Unit III. Press as desired. Make 12 blocks.

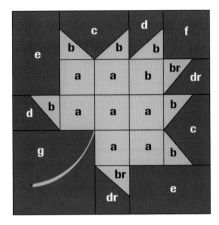

Leaf Block
Make 12.

Quilt Assembly

1. Lay a Leaf block flat, with the stem at the upper right corner. Arrange background blocks *A*, *C*, and *D* around it on three sides, as shown in the upper left corner of the Quilt Assembly diagram. Sew *A* to the top edge of the Leaf block. Press toward *A*. Add *C* to the left side edge and *D* to the bottom edge, pressing after each addition.

2. Repeat Step 1 to assemble the second unit in Row 1 of the Quilt Assembly diagram. Lay out the Leaf block and the appropriate background blocks. Join the background blocks in alphabetical order, skipping over any letters that are missing. Press as you go. Continue in this way until all 12 units are sewn.

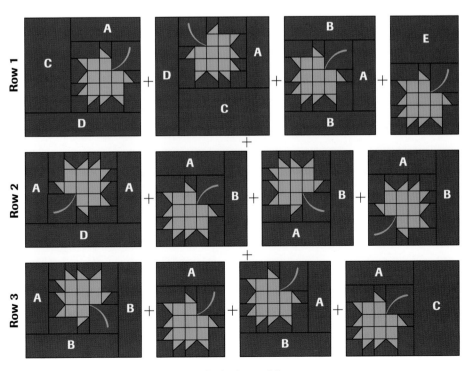

Quilt Assembly

3. Join the units together in rows. Press Rows 1 and 3 in one direction and Row 2 in the opposite direction. Join the rows. Press.

4. Sew the top and bottom inner borders to the quilt top. Press toward the inner borders. Sew the side inner borders to the quilt top. Press toward the inner borders.

5. Sew the top and bottom outer borders to the quilt top. Press toward the inner borders. Sew the side outer borders to the quilt top. Press toward the inner borders.

Finishing

1. Layer and baste the quilt top, batting, and backing.

2. Lay the Flexicurve tool on the upper right corner of the quilt top and shape it into a gentle serpentine curve or swirl. Trace along the curved edge with a fabric marker.

Practice using the Flexicurve design tool ruler on paper before marking your quilt.

3. Quilt the marked line with the traditional stitch (page 37). Use three to four values of perle cotton, in colors that coordinate with the leaf fabrics. Repeat Steps 2 and 3, using a mark-as-you-go approach, to continue the curving lines as desired. Work toward the lower left corner of the quilt.

4. Bind the edges.

Quilting Pattern

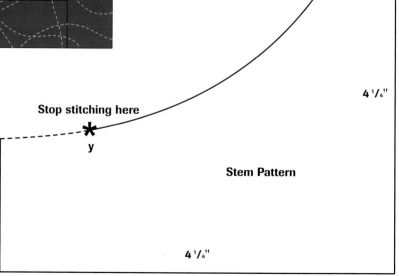

x
Start stitching here

4 ¹/₄"

Stop stitching here
✳
y

Stem Pattern

4 ¹/₄"

Random Hearts

by Linda Potter ◈ 2002, 28" x 58"

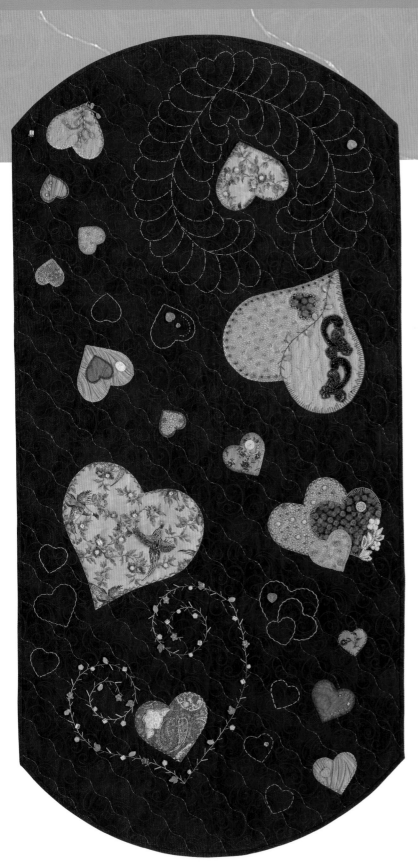

Cotton fabrics, #8 perle cotton, holographic thread, Thermore batting. Hand-appliquéd, hand-quilted, beaded.

Random Hearts *is a table runner, created to evoke the elegant, eclectic style of the Victorian era. Various quilted and appliquéd hearts let you sample every stitching, appliqué, and beading technique I teach in this book. Of particular interest are the large quilted hearts at each end that are designed to embrace smaller heart appliqués. Such perfect marriages are easier to pull off when you plan the embellishment strategy at the beginning of the project.*

The background quilting presented a separate challenge. High-contrast pink and green threads detracted from the hearts, and a matching dark burgundy thread all but disappeared. Wrapping the burgundy stitches with a double strand of holographic machine sewing thread gave me a way to enhance the stitching while retaining delicacy.

Materials

Background and binding: 2 yards
Hearts:
  4 fat quarters
  $1/8$ yard each of 2 to 4 assorted
    fabrics
Backing: $1\,3/4$ yards
Batting: 32" x 62"
Heavy-duty fusible web: 1 yard

You'll also need tracing paper,
an 11" x 17" sheet of template
plastic, and pressing sheets.

Cutting

Prepare plastic templates for the
curved edge and hearts *a*, *b*, *c*,
and *d* (pages 66 and 67).

Background and Binding

❏ Cut 1 rectangle 28" x 58" on
the lengthwise grain. Use the
curved edge template to mark a
curve on each short edge. (Do not
cut the curve until you are ready
to apply the binding.)
❏ Cut the remaining background
fabric into $2\,1/4$"-wide bias strips.
Piece the strips together end to
end to make a binding strip at
least 180" long.

Hearts

❏ Make a placement guide for
bde and *gh* (see Exercise 1, page
46, and the patterns on pages 67
and 68).
❏ Use the heart templates to trace
7 *a*, 4 *b*, 2 *c*, and 3 *d* onto fusible
web. Use the heart patterns (page
67) to trace 1 *f* and 1 *g* onto
fusible web. Use the placement
guide to trace 1 *d*, 1 *e*, and 1 *h*
with extensions.
❏ Cut out each fusible web shape
$1/4$" beyond the marked outline and
$1/8$" inside the marked outline (see
Exercise 3, page 47).
❏ Select a fabric for each heart
shape. Fuse each fusible web
doughnut to the wrong side of the
fabric, following the manufacturer's
instructions. Cut out each appliqué
on the marked outline.

Assembly and Finishing

1. Place the background fabric
right side up.

2. Trim off the fusible web from
the extensions of hearts *d*, *e*, and *h*
(see Exercise 4, page 48). Remove
the paper backing from each heart
shape.

3. Lay out the heart appliqués on
the background fabric, at least 1"
in from the edges and marked
curves, as shown in the Quilt
Diagram (page 65) and quilt
photograph (page 63). Overlap
pieces *g* and *h*, pieces *b*, *d*, and
e, and pieces *a* and *c,* as shown.
When you are satisfied with
the arrangement, pin the hearts
in place.

4. Working in sections, remove
the pins and fuse the hearts in
place. Follow the manufacturer's
pressing instructions.

5. Layer and baste.

6. Refer to Straight Stitches
(page 37) and Decorative Stitches
(page 40) to work the quilted
embellishment. Use a variety of
perle cotton colors that match,
coordinate, and contrast with the
heart and background fabrics to
work the quilting.
❏ Appliqué the hearts using the
herringbone stitch, blanket stitch,
and angled overcast stitch. Add
beads as desired.

❏ Use a stencil to mark a feathered heart or another ornate design at an angle at one end of the table runner. Quilt with the short long stitch.

❏ Mark a stylized heart at an angle on the opposite end. Quilt with the Magic Fern stitch, adding beads as desired.

❏ Use the plastic templates to mark hearts at random throughout the background. Quilt the heart outlines. Wrap the stitches as desired.

❏ Quilt an overall design across the background, using a thread that matches the background color. Wrap the stitches with a double strand of fine holographic thread for subtle enhancement.

7. Bind the edges, following the marked curve at each end. Sew additional beads and trims to the quilt as desired.

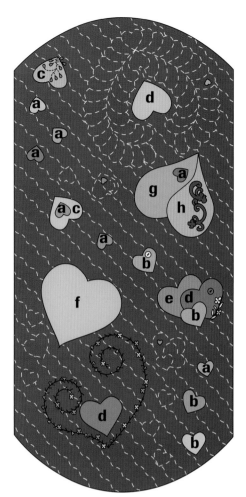

Quilt Diagram

A feathered heart, quilted in short long stitch, embraces a blanket-stitched heart appliqué. Add beads to the blanket stitch as you sew.

The Magic Fern stitch, with beads added during the quilting, creates a swirly quilted heart. The background quilting stitches are wrapped with a double strand of holographic thread.

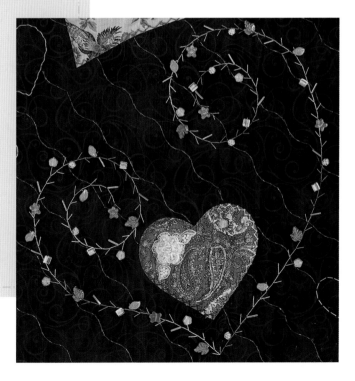

Templates

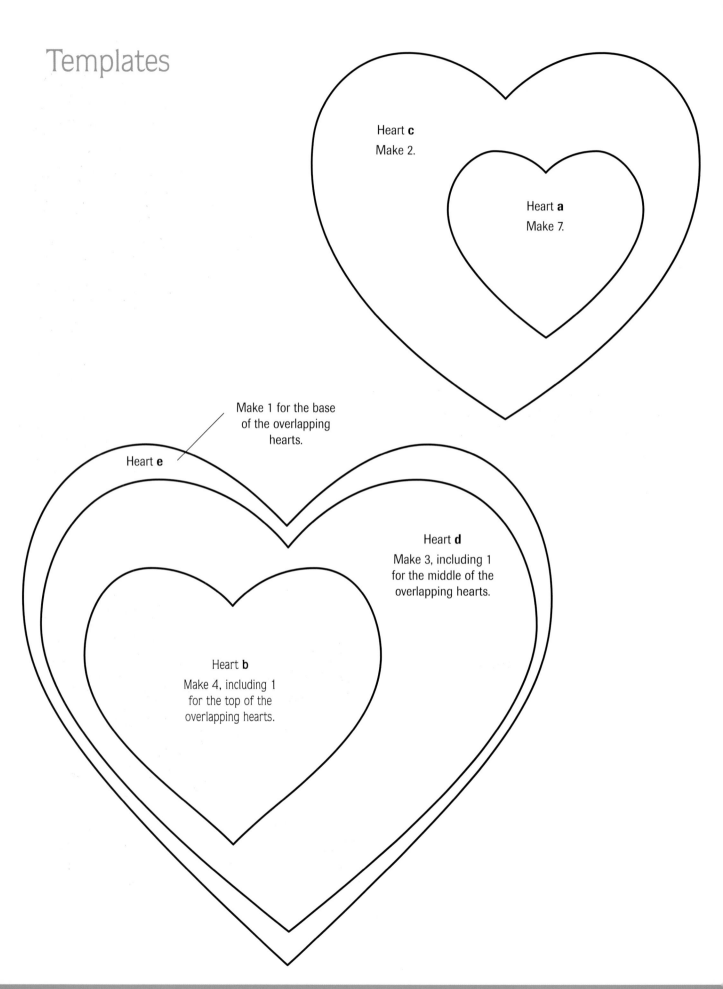

Heart **c**
Make 2.

Heart **a**
Make 7.

Make 1 for the base
of the overlapping
hearts.

Heart **e**

Heart **d**

Make 3, including 1
for the middle of the
overlapping hearts.

Heart **b**

Make 4, including 1
for the top of the
overlapping hearts.

Center

Curve Pattern, one half
Place at short edge of rectangle, and trace curve.
Reverse pattern for opposite side.

Enlarge by 200%.

Long side

Heart **f**
Make 1 of the whole heart.

Heart **h**

Make 1.
Enlarge by 200%.

Heart **g**

Make 1.
Enlarge by 200%.

Heart **gh**
Placement Guide

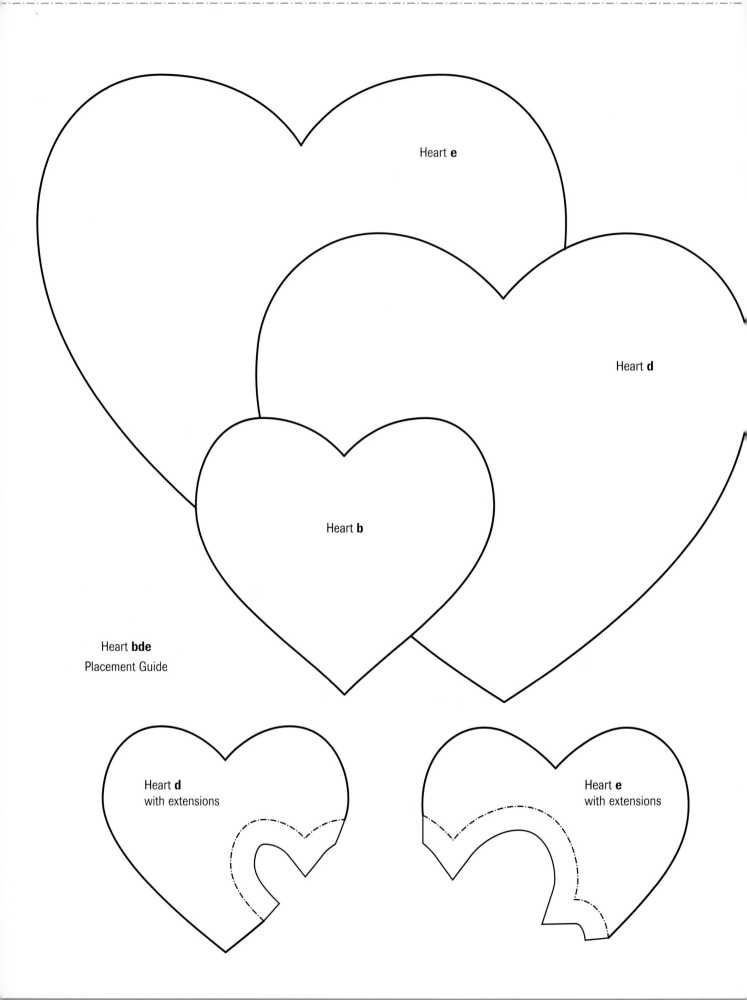

Heart **e**

Heart **d**

Heart **b**

Heart **bde**
Placement Guide

Heart **d**
with extensions

Heart **e**
with extensions

Nagano '98

by Linda Potter ✦ 1998, 45" x 63"

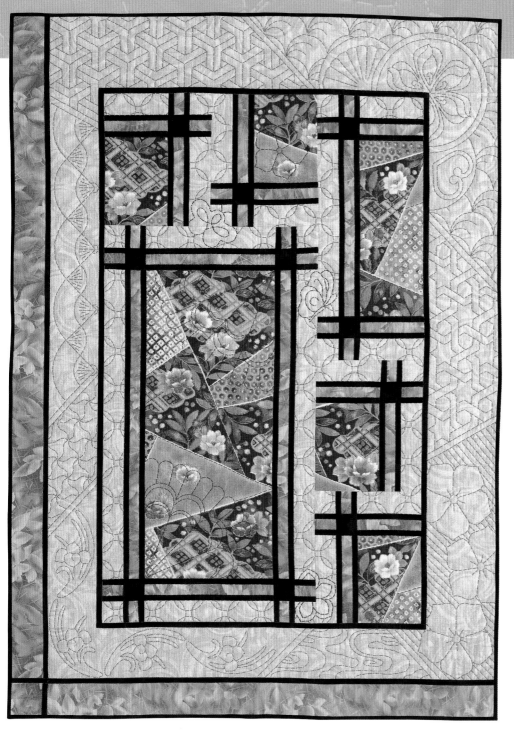

Cotton fabrics, #8 perle cotton, Thermore batting. Machine-pieced, hand-quilted.

The Needle Magic embellishment for this quilt was chosen to re-create the look of traditional Japanese *sashiko* pieces. Instead of white stitching on indigo, I used dark thread on a pale yellow print. I used every Japanese geometric stencil I own, placing the designs at random until I had filled every nook and cranny. A double line of traditional straight stitches separates one pattern from another.

Materials

Theme: $1\frac{1}{2}$ to 2 yards for blocks (the large amount allows for fussy cutting)

Dark Navy: $1\frac{1}{3}$ yards for blocks, borders, and binding

Lavender: 1 yard for blocks and border

Pale Yellow: 2 yards for blocks and border

Backing: 4 yards

Batting: 50" x 70"

Cutting

Theme

❏ Cut 6 rectangles for blocks 1–5 in size order, as listed below. Refer to the individual block diagrams (pages 71–72) and the overall block orientation in the Quilt Diagram (page 73) to fussy cut the fabric or take advantage of a directional design in the print. Label your cut pieces.

　Block 5: 1 rectangle $12\frac{1}{2}$" x $28\frac{1}{2}$". Label as *a*.

　Block 3: 1 rectangle $6\frac{1}{2}$" x $16\frac{1}{2}$". Label as *b*.

　Blocks 1, 2, and 4: 4 rectangles $6\frac{1}{2}$" x $8\frac{1}{2}$". Label as *c*.

Dark Navy

❏ Cut 20 crosswise strips 1" wide. Set aside 12 strips for the block borders. Sew the remaining 8 strips together end to end with bias seams. Subcut the following:

　Border *A*: 2 strips $48\frac{1}{2}$" long

　Border *B*: 2 strips $31\frac{1}{2}$" long

　Border *G*: 1 strip $60\frac{1}{2}$" long

　Border *I*: 1 strip 46" long

　Border *K*: 1 strip $3\frac{1}{2}$" long

❏ Cut 1 crosswise strip $2\frac{1}{2}$" wide. Subcut into 10 squares $2\frac{1}{2}$" x $2\frac{1}{2}$" for the block borders. Label as *d*.

❏ Cut 7 crosswise strips $2\frac{1}{2}$" wide for the binding.

Lavender

❏ Cut 6 crosswise strips $1\frac{1}{2}$" wide for the block borders.

❏ Cut 3 crosswise strips $3\frac{1}{2}$" wide. Sew the strips together end to end with bias seams. Subcut the following:

　Border *H*: $3\frac{1}{2}$" x $60\frac{1}{2}$"

　Border *J*: $3\frac{1}{2}$" x $3\frac{1}{2}$"

　Border *L*: $3\frac{1}{2}$" x $42\frac{1}{2}$"

Pale Yellow

❏ Cut 5 crosswise strips $2\frac{1}{2}$" wide for the block borders.

❏ Cut 4 lengthwise strips:

　Border *C*: 5" x $49\frac{1}{2}$"

　Border *D*: 7" x $49\frac{1}{2}$"

　Border *E*: 7" x $42\frac{1}{2}$"

　Border *F*: 5" x $42\frac{1}{2}$"

Block Borders

Note: Accurate sewing and pressing are critical for the piecing in this quilt. Refer to Making the Quilts (page 92). Press very carefully toward the dark navy fabric.

1. Refer to Strip Sets (page 93). For the main block borders, piece 5 identical strip sets. For each strip set, use these four strips:

　1"-wide dark navy strip

　$1\frac{1}{2}$"-wide lavender strip

　1"-wide dark navy strip

　$2\frac{1}{2}$"-wide pale yellow strip

2. Subcut the 5 strip sets into 5 sections, using 1 strip set per section:

　2 sections $28\frac{1}{2}$" long. Label as *e*.

　1 section $16\frac{1}{2}$" long. Label as *f*.

　2 sections $12\frac{1}{2}$" long. Label as g.

Cut the remainder into the following sections:

　4 sections $8\frac{1}{2}$" long. Label as *h*.

　6 sections $6\frac{1}{2}$" long. Label as *i*.

　10 sections $2\frac{1}{2}$" long. Label as *j*.

3. For the block border corners, piece 1 strip set. Use these strips:

　1"-wide dark navy strip

　$1\frac{1}{2}$"-wide lavender strip

　1"-wide dark navy strip

4. Subcut the block border corners strip set into 10 sections $2\frac{1}{2}$" long. Label as *k*.

Block Assembly

Note: Assemble blocks 1–5 one at a time. Pay particular attention to the orientation of fussy-cut fabrics and the borders in blocks 1, 2, and 4. These blocks are similar in appearance, and it's easy to confuse the pieces. Use a $^1/_4''$ seam allowance. Press all seam allowances toward the dark navy fabric.

1. For Block 1, lay out pieces *c*, *d*, *h*, *i*, *j*, and *k,* as shown. Join the pieces together. Make 2 blocks.

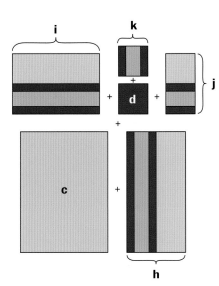

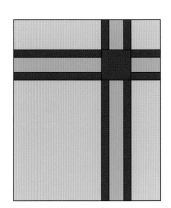

Block 1
Make 2.

2. For Block 2, lay out pieces *c*, *d*, *h*, *i*, *j*, and *k,* as shown. Join the pieces together. Make 1 block.

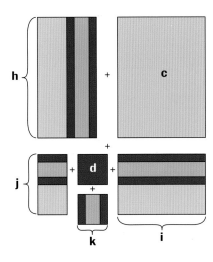

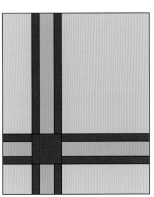

Block 2
Make 1.

3. For Block 3, lay out 1 *b*, 1 *f*, and 2 each of *d*, *i*, *j*, and *k*. Join the pieces together. Make 1 block.

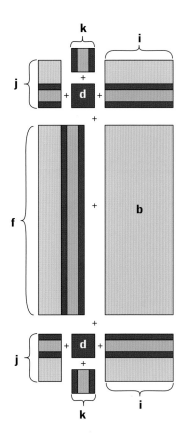

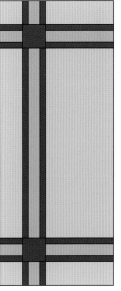

Block 3
Make 1.

4. For Block 4, lay out pieces *c*, *d*, *h*, *i*, *j*, and *k*. Join the pieces together. Make 1 block.

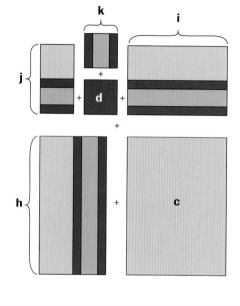

Block 4
Make 1.

5. For Block 5, lay out 1 *a*, 2 *e*, 2 *g*, and 4 each of *d*, *j*, and *k*. Join the pieces together. Make 1 block.

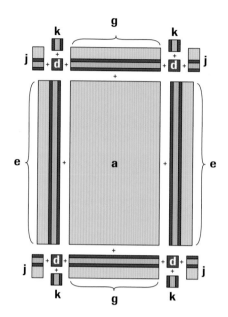

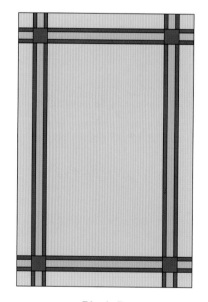

Block 5
Make 1.

Quilt Assembly

1. Lay out blocks 1–5, as shown in the Quilt Diagram. Double-check the orientation of blocks 1, 2, and 4. Stitch Block 1 to Block 2. Press as desired. Add Block 5. Press toward Block 5. Join blocks 3, 1, and 4. Press as desired. Sew the two block units together. Press toward the block 1/2/5 unit.

2. Sew the *A* border strips to each side edge of the quilt top. Press toward *A*. Sew the *B* strips to the top and bottom edges. Press toward *B*.

3. Sew Border *C* to the left edge of the quilt top. Press toward *A*. Sew Border *D* to the right edge of the quilt top. Press toward *A*. Sew Border *E* to the top edge of the quilt top. Press toward *B*. Sew Border *F* to the bottom edge of the quilt top. Press toward *B*.

4. Sew borders *G* and *H* together. Press toward *G*. Sew the *GH* unit to the left edge of the quilt top, with *G* on the inside. Press toward *G*. Sew Border *I* to the bottom edge of the quilt top. Press toward *I*.

5. Sew borders *J*, *K*, and *L* together. Press both seam allowances toward *K*. Sew the *JKL* unit to the bottom edge of the quilt top, with *J* at the lower left corner. Press toward *I*.

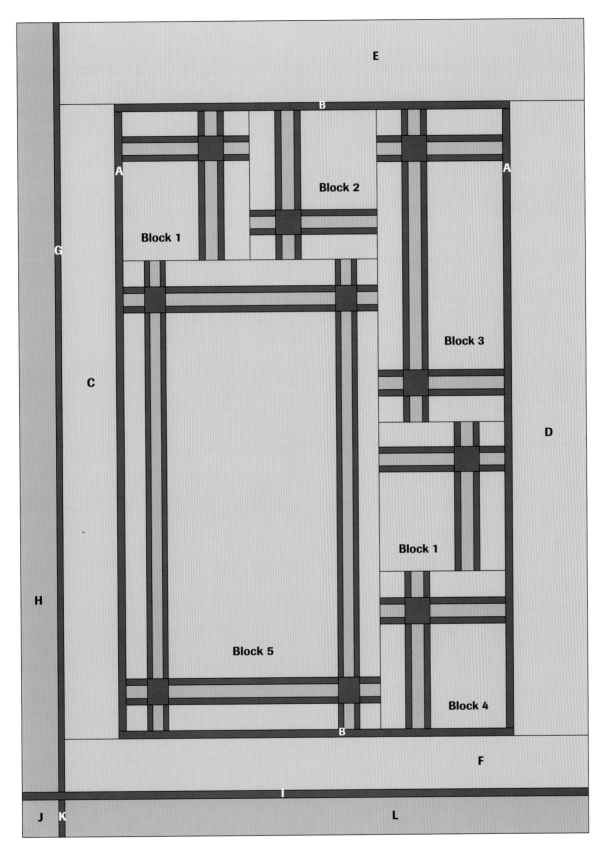

Quilt Assembly

Finishing

1. Layer and baste.

2. Use stencils to mark assorted oriental-style designs on the quilt top.

■ Suggested motifs are fans, lotus blossoms, and *sashiko*-style interlocking geometric patterns.

■ Refer to the quilt photograph (page 69) for suggested stencil placements.

■ Mark two parallel diagonal lines $^1/_2$" apart to separate the patterns.

3. Work the quilted embellishment in traditional stitch (page 37) using perle cotton.

■ Choose colors of perle cotton that contrast with the fabrics for the oriental designs.

■ Quilt in-the-ditch along the contrasting block and border strips. Use a thread color that matches the dark navy fabric.

4. Bind the edges to add a final $^1/_2$"-wide dark navy band around the entire quilt.

Closely spaced parallel stitching lines separate three different designs on the quilt border.

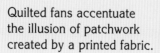

Quilted fans accentuate the illusion of patchwork created by a printed fabric.

Night Flight

by Linda Potter ✤ 2003, 54" x 39"

Night Flight *demonstrates how a variety of patterned fabrics can still allow for visible embellishment. During the piecing phase, I thought naturally of quilting additional stars for the background. As I searched through my stencil collection, however, I found stencils for fluttering butterflies and cattails, and the design progressed from there.*

Cotton fabrics, #8 perle cotton, Thermore batting. Machine-pieced, hand-quilted, beaded.

Materials

Background: 7 to 14 assorted fat quarters

Stars: 7 assorted fat quarters (or $1/4$-yard cuts)

Border: $1^3/4$ yards

Binding: $1/2$ yard

Backing: $1^3/4$ yards

Batting: 43" x 59"

Cutting

Background

❏ Cut 34 assorted lengthwise strips $3^1/2$" x 18". Subcut at random into:

　1 rectangle $3^1/2$" x $15^1/2$". Label as **a**.

　7 rectangles $3^1/2$" x $12^1/2$". Label as **b**.

　9 rectangles $3^1/2$" x $9^1/2$". Label as **c**.

　14 rectangles $3^1/2$" x $6^1/2$". Label as **d**.

　31 squares $3^1/2$" x $3^1/2$". Label as **e**.

　32 rectangles $3^1/2$" x 2". Label as **f**.

　24 squares 2" x 2". Label as **g**.

Stars

❏ Cut 7 assorted squares $3^1/2$" x $3^1/2$" for the large star centers. Label as **h**.

❏ Cut 8 assorted squares 2" x 2" for the small star centers. Label as **i**.

❏ Cut 7 assorted strips 2" x 17". Subcut each strip into 8 squares 2" x 2" for the large star points. Label as **j**.

❏ Cut 8 assorted strips $1^1/4$" x 11". Subcut each strip into 8 squares $1^1/4$" x $1^1/4$" for the small star points. Label as **k**.

Border

❏ Cut 4 lengthwise strips 5" wide. Subcut into:

　2 strips 5" x $54^1/2$" for the top and bottom borders.

　2 strips 5" x $30^1/2$" for the side borders.

Assembly

A design wall placed near the sewing machine will help you arrange and keep track of the background pieces as you sew.

1. Lay out pieces **a** through **i** on a design wall, as shown in the Quilt Assembly diagram (page 77). Reposition the blocks to design your own arrangement, if desired. Note how pieces **f** and **g** are used to fill out the area around the small star centers **i**.

2. For each large star center **h**, select 8 matching **j** squares for the contrasting star points. Use the Connector method (page 93) to sew 2 **j** squares to each square or rectangle that will share a seam with **h**. Return the pieces to the design wall.

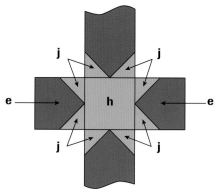

Large Star Points

3. For each small star center **i**, select 8 matching **k** squares for the contrasting star points. Use the Connector method to sew 2 **k** squares to each square or rectangle that will share a seam with **i**. Return the pieces to the design wall.

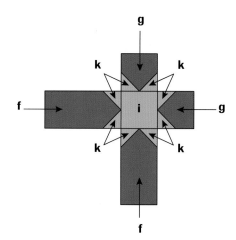

Small Star Points

4. Sew the pieces together in columns. Make 15 columns total. Press the small star seam allowances toward the center of the star. Press the other seams as desired. Sew the columns together. Press.

5. Sew the top and bottom borders to the quilt top. Press toward the borders. Sew the side borders to the quilt top. Press toward the borders.

Finishing

1. Layer and baste.

2. Refer to Traditional Stitch and Short Long Stitch (page 37) to work the quilted embellishment. Use colors of perle cotton that contrast sharply against the star and background colors.

■ Quilt in-the-ditch around each star using perle cotton that matches the stars.

■ Quilt the background and borders at random, using various star, butterfly, bird, and dragonfly designs, adding beads as desired.

3. Bind the edges.

4. Sew on beads and sequins as desired to add glitz and sparkle.

Quilting Pattern

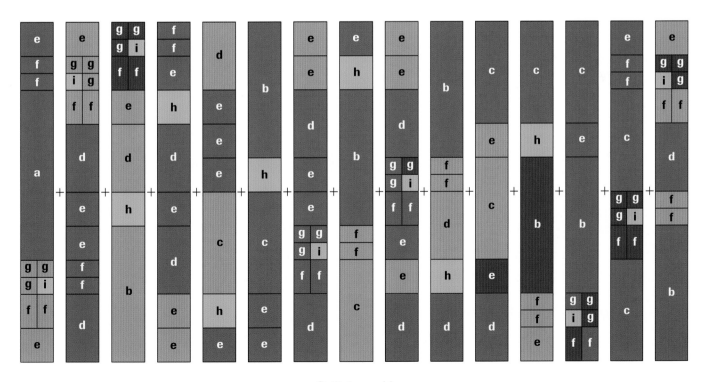

Quilt Assembly

Gallery

My Dream Vacation

by Judy Oberkrom and
Linda Potter
2003, 27" x 30"

Batik fabrics, #8 perle
cotton, beads, Thermore
batting. Machine-pieced,
machine-appliquéd, hand-
quilted, beaded.

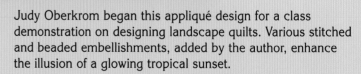

Judy Oberkrom began this appliqué design for a class
demonstration on designing landscape quilts. Various stitched
and beaded embellishments, added by the author, enhance
the illusion of a glowing tropical sunset.

Top right: Beads added after quilting give definition to the
palm frond silhouettes. Large beads became coconuts.

Bottom left: Three concentric arcs accentuate the pulsating
sunset. Each arc is worked in traditional stitch and wrapped
with beads. An explosion of seed stitches in fiery colors
intensifies the sun interior. The mood below is much calmer,
where short long stitch is the key to gently curving lines that
represent water currents. The fish-shaped bead was added
during quilting.

Citron Explosion

by Charlotte Gurwell
2003, 34" x 34"

Cotton and hand-painted cotton fabrics,
#8 perle cotton, beads, batting.
Machine-pieced, hand-quilted, beaded.

The artist designed this richly textured piece around her own hand-painted fabric square. The flamelike designs emanating from the center are worked in traditional stitch. The dense areas of quilting are done in seed stitch, a technique where running stitches are worked in random directions. The broad rings of color around the center medallion are actually hundreds of tiny hand-worked stitches.

Leanne's Mirage

by Kathy Delaney
2002, 61" x 48"

Hand-dyed cotton fabrics, #5 perle cotton, Thermore batting. Machine-pieced, hand-quilted.

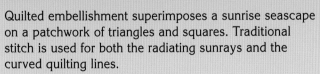

Quilted embellishment superimposes a sunrise seascape on a patchwork of triangles and squares. Traditional stitch is used for both the radiating sunrays and the curved quilting lines.

Right: Detail of the quilted sun and sunrays. Variegated hand-dyed threads were used.

Whig Rose II

by Linda Potter
1997, 56" x 56"

Cotton fabrics, #5 and #8 perle cotton,
Thermore batting. Hand-appliquéd,
machine-pieced, hand-quilted.

The appliqué and floral quilting are
worked in herringbone stitch and angled
overcast stitch using thick, colorful
threads. The quilted floral designs echo
the motifs found in the appliqués while
cutting down on the overall stitching
time. The lattice designs in the background are quilted in traditional stitch
and short long stitch. Done in ecru
thread, this quilting is visible but does
not compete with the appliqués, for a
more subtle presence.

Whig Rose

by Linda Potter
1997, 39" x 39"

Cotton fabrics, #8 perle cotton,
cotton batting. Machine-pieced,
hand-appliquéd, hand-quilted.

The appliqué edges are
stitched with hand-dyed
perle cotton, ranging in
color from burgundy to
green. Intermittent touches
of light olive green in
the thread add surprise
highlights. The subtle
tone-on-tone light gray
background print is
quilted with a gray-green
thread. This combination
keeps the eye moving
without creating a lot of
commotion. The entire quilt reads as "traditional" from
a distance but delivers a totally different perspective
the closer you get.

Serenity

by Linda Potter
2002, 57 1/2" x 57 1/2"

Cotton fabrics, #8 perle cotton, beads, Thermore batting. Machine-pieced, hand-appliquéd, hand-quilted, beaded. Adapted from a Robyn Pandolph quilt pattern by the same name.

A stunning floral motif is appliquéd with herringbone, Myrtle, and angled overcast stitches. Butterflies quilted in burgundy and green threads fill in the blank spaces around the edges. The border is heavily quilted with a series of radiating arcs in a green thread that blends in. The butterflies are worked in short long stitch, and the arcs are worked in traditional stitch.

Evening Lillies

by Linda Potter
2000, 33" x 54"

Cotton and batik fabrics, #8 perle cotton, Thermore batting.
Machine-pieced, hand-appliquéd, hand-quilted, beaded.

This design combines dimensional flowers and leaves with appliquéd stems. Grassy tendrils dance across the background. The grass is quilted in Magic Fern stitch with variegated green thread. Some viewers see tropical fish instead of flowers, and seaweed instead of grass. Which do you see, flowers or fish?

Detail: The loose folded edge is flipped back on itself and tacked down with a bead. This curved edge treatment was inspired by the "twiddling and fiddling" work of Jennie Rayment, a quiltmaker known for her creative fabric manipulation.

The Splendid Poppy

by Linda Potter
2002, 35" x 35"

Cotton fabrics, #8 and #5 perle cotton,
Thermore batting. Machine-pieced, machine-
appliquéd, hand-quilted. The appliqué is a
Kathy Delaney design from the book *Hearts
and Flowers* (*Kansas City Star*, 2002).

Mirror images are worked in short long stitch in
each corner of this quilt, mimicking the large
appliqué design at the center. The thread colors
relate to the appliqué fabrics.

Fractured Snowballs

by Linda Potter and Charlotte Gurwell
2003, 67" x 67"

Cotton fabrics, #8 perle cotton, cotton
batting. Machine-pieced, machine- and
hand-quilted, beaded.

Rather than quilt the same
design in every block, the
author took advantage of the
purposely obscure machine
quilting, completed by Charlotte
Gurwell, to concentrate the
embellishment in selected areas.

Star Spangled

by Ilyse Moore
2003, 18" x 24"

Cotton fabrics, variegated perle cotton,
metallic thread, buttons, Thermore batting.
Hand-appliquéd, hand-quilted.

This small, triangular banner, designed for a
contest at Prairie Point, uses traditional and
dimensional appliqués to create firecrackers that
pop! Traditional stitch, blanket stitch, and other
embroidery stitches add to the collage effect.
Metallic stitching accents the background.

Stairway to the Stars

by Linda Potter
2001, 69" x 81"

Cotton fabrics, #8 perle cotton, Thermore batting. Machine-pieced, hand-quilted. Inspired by an antique quilt top owned by Barbara Brackman.

Without actually depicting a flag, rippling quilting lines create the impression that Old Glory is waving in the breeze. The background and borders are quilted with wiggly lines. Star templates were used for the appliqués as well as for the quilted star shapes. Both ecru and dark blue threads were used.

Falling Leaves

by Karen Hansen
2001, 46" x 54"

Cotton and batik fabrics, #8 perle cotton, Thermore batting. Machine-pieced, machine-appliquéd, machine- and hand-quilted. Adapted from Linda Potter's pattern Stairway to the Stars.

Freestyle quilting lines wend their way among appliquéd leaves to suggest gusts of wind. The traditional stitch quilting lines are widely spaced and mostly decorative, since the entire piece was machine-quilted as well.

Delightfully Victorian

by Linda Potter
1996, 54 ¹/₄" x 69 ¹/₂"

Cotton fabrics, #8 perle cotton, Thermore
batting. Machine-pieced, hand-quilted.

Thread and fabric colors energize
one another in this rich, complex
Victorian palette. The stars and
the block edges are accented with
traditional stitch and Magic Fern
stitch in a seemingly endless
selection of colors; all designed to
contribute to a harmonious whole.

40 Shades of Color

by Connie Coffman
2001, 47" x 57 ½"

Batik fabrics, #8 perle cotton, polyester batting.
Machine-pieced, hand-quilted.

Assorted perle cotton threads accent the jewel-like colors of this crazy quilt patchwork. The artist experimented with a variety of embroidery stitches to quilt the layers together.

Let the Sun Shine In

by Linda Potter
2003, 60" x 60"

Cotton fabrics, #8 perle cotton, Thermore
batting. Machine-pieced, hand-quilted.

A half-round sun design, quilted in yellow thread, fills
the large setting triangles of this medallion-style quilt.
Traditional stitch quilting in the border follows the
fabric print. The patchwork is quilted in-the-ditch.

Double Star Twist

by Jeanne Poore
2000, 51" x 59"

Cotton fabrics, #8 perle cotton, Thermore
batting. Machine-pieced, hand-quilted.

Medallion-style quilts typically feature large, open
areas that are perfect for quilted embellishment.
This quilting design, worked in traditional stitch,
adds to the movement of the blocks. The teal thread
color picks up on the border theme print.

Moon Glow

by Dorothy Larsen
2003, 40" x 40"

Cotton and organza fabrics, #8 perle cotton, beads, Thermore
batting. Machine-pieced, hand-quilted, hand-appliquéd, beaded.

The quiltmaker designed floral and vine appliqués
and a sheer "moonbeam" overlay to create this
midnight garden. Short long stitch quilting repeats
the vine's leaf motif in yellow and pink threads.
The background was pieced in a class taught by
Connie Pomering.

Redwork Ladies Floral Baskets

by Patricia Spencer and Jeanne Poore
2003, 75" x 79"

Cotton fabrics, #8 perle cotton, Thermore batting. Machine-pieced, hand-embroidered, hand-quilted.

This quilter's classic was adapted from a 1930s muslin-stamped pattern from Home Art Studio of Des Moines, Iowa. The blocks are embroidered by hand with red floss. Feathered scrolls are quilted in the border with red perle cotton, for a new twist on an old favorite.

Elegant Embellishments

by Linda Potter
2001, 39" x 39"

Batik fabrics, #8 perle cotton, metallic thread, Thermore batting. Machine-pieced, hand-quilted, beaded.

The author used rich, dark stitching to visually separate and define two medium-value patchwork fabrics. In this sampler quilt, herringbone stitch, blanket stitch, and Myrtle stitch in-the-ditch accent the patchwork shapes. Stitching with a light color and wrapping with a dark color creates a striking effect in the center of the quilt. Another interesting stitch effect is the alternating rows of Magic Fern stitch and short long stitch accented with beads.

Midnight Stars

by Carol Kirchhoff and Linda Potter
2001, 51" x 51"

Cotton fabrics, #8 perle cotton, Thermore batting. Machine-pieced, hand-quilted.

Carol Kirchhoff pieced this quilt using the Winged Square block originally published in the *Kansas City Star*. The author added the quilted embellishment—a galaxy of stars worked in short long stitch in an exaggerated shade of variegated yellow-green, for maximum contrast against the blue background. The quilt is featured in the book *Kansas City Quiltmakers* (Kansas City Star, 2001).

Pumpkin Party

by Linda Potter
2003, 52" x 66"

Cotton fabrics, #8 perle cotton, Thermore batting.
Machine-pieced, hand-appliquéd, hand-quilted.

The author pieced this quilt while she anxiously
awaited word from C&T on her book proposal. A
"yes" answer inspired the exuberant, celebratory
quilting style and the quilt title as well. The pumpkins
are appliquéd with the angled overcast, herringbone,
blanket, and Myrtle stitches. The background swirls
are quilted in traditional stitch in assorted green,
yellow, and orange thread colors.

Japanese Fans

by Barbara Fife
2003, 79" x 56"

Cotton fabrics, #8 perle cotton, Thermore batting. Machine-pieced, hand-quilted, hand-appliquéd. Adapted from the Linda Potter pattern A Touch of the Orient. This quilt won the second viewer's choice award at the Olathe Quilt Guild Show 2004 in Olathe, Kansas.

This festive quilt celebrates the marriage of the quiltmaker's son. The hand-appliquéd fans feature herringbone stitch around the edges and Magic Fern stitch between the fan blades. The crisscrossing curved lines in the background are quilted in traditional stitch. Variegated thread was used throughout.

Making
the Quilts

The four quilt projects in this book are geared to quilters of all levels. In addition to fabric and batting, you'll need perle cotton, threads for wrapping, and beads. Since embellishing is such a creative, intuitive process, and the threads are not expensive, no attempt was made to itemize specific thread colors or amounts. The quilt finishing instructions provide ideas for embellishment.

If you need help with basic quiltmaking skills, such as layering, basting, or binding your quilt, ask at your local quilt shop or consult one of the quilting guides listed in For Further Reading (page 94). Here are some general guidelines to keep in mind as you begin each project.

Fabric

▓ All yardages are calculated for a 40" width and are rounded up to the next $^1/_4$ yard.

▓ The yardage calculation for the quilt backing allows for a vertical seam, where required.

▓ A fat quarter measures 18" x 20".

Cutting

▓ Use the project cutting instructions as a ☑ checklist, not an itinerary. Some quilters like to cut everything at the beginning, and others like to cut and sew in stages. I like to wait until the quilt top is completed before cutting any border strips. That way, I can measure the quilt top and cut the exact sizes I need.

▓ For a crosswise strip, cut across the width of the fabric, from selvage to selvage.

▓ For a lengthwise strip, cut along the length of the fabric.

▓ "Subcut" means to cut a strip or strip set into smaller sections, as specified.

▓ Use plastic templates to mark and cut appliqué shapes. See Exercise 2 on page 46 to make your own plastic templates.

Piecing and Pressing

▦ Use a $1/4$" seam allowance.

▦ Press after each piecing sequence. To avoid stretching and distorting the fabric, be sure to press only; do not iron.

▦ Press toward the darker fabric unless otherwise noted.

▦ Use bias seams to join strips for borders and bindings. Press bias seams open. Subcut the strips into smaller sections as directed.

▦ The dimensions on the quilt block, unit, and quilt diagrams indicate the size after piecing. They do not include the $1/4$" seam allowance. Finished quilt dimensions do not include the binding.

▦ Do not fuse appliqué shapes to the quilt top prematurely, or they may come loose and fall off. Fuse them immediately before you baste the quilt top.

Strip Sets

Use this technique to speed up the piecing process. Sew two or more strips together along the long edges to make a strip set. Press. Then cut the strip set into smaller units.

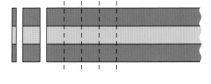

Strip Sets

Connector

Use this method, developed by Mary Ellen Hopkins, to piece seams at a 45° angle. Cut a fabric square (the connector) and another piece of fabric (square or rectangle), as the project instructions direct. Place the connector on the corner of the other piece of fabric, right sides together with the corners matching. Stitch diagonally from corner to corner, as shown. Trim off only the corner of the connector $1/4$" from the stitching line.

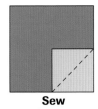

Sew

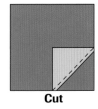

Cut

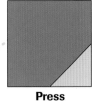

Press

Connector Method

Double-Fold Binding

Cut the binding strips $2 1/4$" wide, or as directed, and piece them together end to end with bias seams to obtain the required length. Press the seams open. Fold the strip in half lengthwise, right side out, and press. Match the raw edges of the binding to the raw edge of the quilt top. Machine-stitch $1/4$" from the edge, or as directed, mitering the corners as you go. When you reach the starting point, join the ends together with a bias seam and trim off the excess. Trim away the excess batting and backing fabric even with the raw edge of the quilt top. Then fold the binding onto the back of the quilt and tack in place by hand. This binding can also be sewn to the reverse side, folded to the front of the quilt, and tacked with a decorative stitch.

Resources

Make your local quilt and needle-work shop your first stop for quilt-making and embellishment supplies. If they don't stock what you need, try national craft and hobby retailers or the vendors below.

Bag Lady Press
P.O. Box 2409
Evergreen, CO 80437-2409
888-222-4523
www.baglady.com
Finca perle cotton under the
Presencia logo.

The Caron Collection
203-381-9999
www.caron-net.com
Variegated perle cotton and other
designer threads.

The Colonial Needle Co.
74 Westmoreland Road
White Plains, NY 10606
914-946-7474
www.colonialneedle.com
Visit the online shop for needles
and thimbles.

The Electric Quilt Company
419 Gould Street, Suite 2
Bowling Green OH 43047
800-356-4219
www.electricquilt.com
Electric Quilt 5 (EQ5) quilt design
software.

Morgan Hoops & Stands, Inc.
P.O. Box 974
High Ridge, MO 63049-0974
636-376-3800
www.nosliphoops.com
Nonslip quilting hoops.

Prairie Point
7341 Quivira Road
Shawnee, KS 66210
913-268-3333
www.prairiepoint.com
My favorite local quilt shop. Visit the
website.

Quilting Creations International, Inc.
P.O. Box 512
Zoar, OH 44697
330-874-4741
www.quiltingcreations.com
A wide selection of plastic quilting
stencils.

Roxanne International
295 W. Louise Avenue
Manteca, CA 95336
800-993-4445
www.thatperfectstitch.com
Visit the online shop for needles
and thimbles.

The Stencil Company
28 Castlewood Drive, Dept. WW
Cheektowaga, NY 14227
716-656-9430
www.quiltingstencils.com
A wide selection of plastic quilting
stencils.

StenSource International Inc.
800-642-9293
www.stensource.com
A wide selection of plastic quilting
stencils.

For Further Reading

The Art of Classic Quiltmaking
Harriet Hargrave and Sharon Craig
C&T Publishing, 2000
The ultimate how-to book for quilters.

Beaded Embellishment
Amy C. Clarke & Robin Atkins
Interweave Press, 2002
Informational reading for beading on fabric.

Color Play
Joen Wolfrom
C&T Publishing, 2000
Creative exercises to broaden your color
experience and stretch your imagination.

Color: The Quilters' Guide
Christine Barnes
That Patchwork Place, 1997
Find out how colors interact with and
affect one another and then build a
color scheme that works for you.

Elegant Stitches
Judith Montano
C&T Publishing, 1995
Illustrations and instructions for
working both traditional and silk ribbon
embroidery. This book is a little treasure!

A Fine Line
Melody Crust and Heather Waldron Terwell
The Quilt Digest Press, 2002
Learn how to use the principles of
design—shape, line, color, proportion—
to create a quilting design that is
appropriate to the quilt.

Floral Ornament
Carol Belanger Grafton
Dover Publications, Inc., 1977
Floral designs that can be enlarged and
adapted for Needle Magic.

Infinite Feathers
Anita Shackelford
American Quilters Society, 2002
A step-by-step guide to creating
feathered quilting designs in any size.

Japanese Country Quilting
Karen Kim Matsunaga
Kodansa International Ltd., 1990
An introductory look at the design and
application of the art of *sashiko*.

Off the Beadin Path
Nancy Eha
Self-published, 2002
A self-help guide to beading on fabric.

Quilting with Japanese Fabrics
Kitty Pippen
That Patchwork Place, 2000
Designing quilts with Japanese fabrics.

Quilt Marking
Pepper Cory
C&T Publishing, 1999
Learn how to choose quilting designs, fit
designs to the quilt, and make quilt
stencils. Discover new tools and methods for marking a quilt for hand quilting.

*Sashiko Blue and White Quilt Art of
Japan*
Kazuko Mende and Reiko Morishige
Shufunotomo Co., Ltd., 1991
An inspiring pictorial display of modern
sashiko pieces.

That Perfect Stitch
Roxanne McElroy
Quilt Digest Press, 1998
The definitive reference for the hand
quilter. Includes reviews of various
quilting tools and discusses the ins and
outs of efficient ergonomic quilting.

Treasury of Crazy Quilt Stitches
Carole Samples
American Quilters Society, 1999
A magnificent array of embroidery
designs and motifs.

About
the Author

Linda Potter is an award-winning quilt artist and teacher who has been active in the quilting world since 1981. She has taught beginning quiltmaking classes to almost 1,000 students, has given hundreds of workshops, and travels extensively to lecture and teach her Needle Magic techniques to quilt guilds around the country. Linda has coordinated major guild quilt shows, served as president of the Austin Area Quilt Guild, and presided over the Heartland Quilt Network. As the education coordinator for Prairie Point, a quilt store in Shawnee, Kansas, she is the driving force behind the shop's popular, technically oriented classes. She continues to take classes herself and to make and exhibit quilts. Quilt & Embellish in One Step! is her first book.

Index